FINANCIAL FREEDOM BLUEPRINT

"Mastering the Art of Wealth Building, Strategic Investing, and Smart Money Management for a Life of Financial Independence"

Joseph L. Wolford

Disclaimer:

The information contained in this book is for general informational purposes only. The author, Joseph L. Wolford, is not a financial advisor, and the content within does not constitute professional financial advice. The author disclaims any liability for any loss or damage arising directly or indirectly from the use of the information provided.

While every effort has been made to ensure the accuracy and completeness of the information presented, the author makes no representations or warranties of any kind, express or implied, about the completeness, accuracy, reliability, suitability, or availability concerning the content, graphics, and opinions contained in this book. Any reliance you place on such information is strictly at your own risk.

The book is intended to provide general information on personal finance, investing, and related topics. Readers are encouraged to consult with qualified financial professionals for advice tailored to their individual circumstances.

The author assumes no responsibility for errors or omissions in the content of the book. The inclusion of any links does not necessarily imply a recommendation or endorsement of the views expressed within them.

Table Of Content

INTRODUCTION

Definition of Financial Freedom

In a world dominated by financial pressures, unrelenting debts, and the perpetual pursuit of stability, the concept of financial freedom stands as a beacon of hope and empowerment. But what does it truly mean to be financially free?

Attaining financial freedom is an objective for most individuals. When we talk about being financially free, we often mean that we have sufficient savings, investments, and cash on hand to be able to finance the sort of life that we want for ourselves and our children. It entails the accumulation of funds that will allow us to retire or follow the vocation of our choice without being constrained by the need of earning a certain wage each year. The term "financial freedom" refers to a situation in which our money is working for us but not the other way around.

Picture a life where the perpetual cycle of living paycheck to paycheck is replaced by a sense of security and abundance. Envision a reality where money is a tool that empowers rather than restricts, where the decisions you make are driven by your desires and values rather than financial constraints. This is the promise of financial freedom.

Throughout this endeavor to attain financial independence, we shall examine the foundational tenets that dictate our fiscal existence, scrutinize tactics for prudent money management, and reveal the avenues through which enduring wealth can be accumulated. It is not enough to simply increase one's earnings; one must also comprehend and optimize their relationship with money.

Bear in mind that attaining financial independence is an individual pilgrimage, devoid of a universally applicable methodology. A combination of knowledge, discipline, and a mentality transformation are necessary. Throughout the pages that follow, we will chart a course to help you create your own Financial Freedom Blueprint—one that corresponds with your unique goals, values, and vision for the future

Importance of Financial Freedom

The financially free individual who stays financially free has done something well. They may not have done everything correctly, and may undoubtedly continue to make the odd error, but they're doing a lot right. It's not simple to become financially free or remain that way.

1: Increased Choices

Financial independence, plain and simple, provides us more options. More options of where to buy food, what sort of employment to perform, where to live, where to send our children to school, and much more. The financially free individual may not take advantage of all those possibilities, but the alternatives are there.

For example, a financially free individual may choose to work in a field that brings greater happiness than someone who is living paycheck to paycheck. They get to select their hours, many of the duties they wish to undertake, and what area of the nation to work in.

2: Ability to Play the Long Game

Number two on the significance of financial independence is the capacity to play the long game. The financially free individual is in a position to make judgments based on long-term outlooks. Not merely the short-term objective of day to day survival and taking care of fundamental requirements.

Case in point is someone who takes on a job at a small firm or launches their own business. They may not earn as much at the beginning as if they were working for a huge firm, but there may be a far larger potential.

There's the chance of shorter hours spent in the future, more money to be earned, control over systems put in place, etc.

3: Values Aligned with Spending

Unless they inherited a significant quantity of money or got fortunate, the financially free people usually have made good judgments in the past. More than likely their principles are also linked with their expenditures. This is a point not to be emphasized.

When our ideals are linked with our expenditures, we obtain enhanced clarity. We utilize our money exclusively for basics and items we value, and nothing else. Nothing is wasted, yet there is also no deprivation, or a sensation of missing out. That suggests there is financial balance,

4: Fresh Outlook

With financial independence comes a new viewpoint. Decisions are decided on principles, lifestyle, and life objectives rather than money. The money aspect is still significant to the financially liberated individual, but it's not the driving force. Because money is already taken care of, it doesn't have to be the decisive factor in everything.

That doesn't imply the financially liberated individual can go wild and start purchasing everything in sight. That's a simple way to shift from financially free to not financially free. It basically implies that considerations other than money will weigh higher in the decision making process. It's why a person in this scenario may switch from a high stress profession that pays well to a lower stress one that doesn't pay as well.

5: Less Stress

Money is a very strong word. For people in a hard financial circumstance, the phrase alone may elicit tension, dread, and apprehension. That's where the necessity of financial independence comes into play. The financially liberated individual could have many other things to obsess about, but money isn't one of them.

Sure, we're all going to worry when our kids are out late with pals or if a loved one falls ill. And many things we obsess over are beyond our control. But money is something that can be reigned in. This develops gradually over time but it's a really strong notion that is more than just money.

6: Feeling of Accomplishment

Often forgotten is the sensation of success. This isn't something that shows up on the balance sheet, but it is still substantial. Life isn't just about money or reaching financial benchmarks.

A huge part of life is putting your mind to something, creating a goal, taking steps to fulfill the objective–and then attaining the goal. There's a sense of pleasure and success that comes with it. Think about a sports team that wins the championship in a professional sport.

There are bonuses and other financial incentives that come with the title, but the major purpose for investing the hours in the weight room, practice field, and film room is for the triumph and championship itself. That sensation of achievement. Same applies for reaching a goal–whether it be financial, athletic, professional, family, etc.

7: What You Become in the Process

The value of financial independence isn't only financial. In addition to the feeling of success written about in the previous section, obtaining financial independence is just as much about what you become in the process.

In order to obtain financial independence, you must grow better in the process. Jim Rohn stated "Set goals not for the outcome itself, but for who you get to become in the process." Unless you inherited a bundle of money or won the lottery, there is no way around this.

You have to become better or the financial benefit of financial freedom will not come to fruition. That includes developing new skills, moving beyond your comfort zone, attempting new things, and taking measured risks. Meeting and conquering problems helps you develop as a person, and it's logical that your financial account will expand parallel to that.

8: Increased Confidence

As you fulfill your objectives, it's normal for confidence to rise. When you set a goal like gaining financial independence, then realize it–confidence skyrockets. You've put your mind on a long-term objective and attained it. That's a major thing, and a significant triumph.

The value of reaching a goal like financial independence also gives you the courage to establish other large objectives. You've already fulfilled a fairly huge financial objective, so why not aim for larger things? It doesn't even have to be in the personal finance arena. It might be health, family, travel, or any other form of objective.

It actually doesn't matter what the new objective is since you have the faith you can attain it. Many individuals spend a lifetime attempting to obtain financial independence and don't accomplish it. You've already attained it and may now set your eyes on additional milestones.

9: Improved Relationships

Money conflicts are commonly regarded as one of the leading reasons of divorce in the United States. Gaining financial independence isn't a guarantee to settle all money disputes but it undoubtedly helps. And not merely because financial independence has been realized.

It's also what has occurred in the past to come to financial independence. If a couple has gained financial independence, something right has occurred along the road. There surely have been ebbs and flows and hurdles, and maybe even a few money disagreements–but a lot has gone well to attain financial independence.

A couple that has gained financial independence together has gone through the fire and come out on top. They not only gain the advantages of financial independence, but also the reward of conquering the hardships and obstacles it required to get there. When it occurs spontaneously, the win is all the sweeter.

10: Financial Harmony

Last but not least, the significance of financial independence is attaining financial balance. Financial peace isn't necessary about being "rich" or "wealthy." It's about a sense that you have enough and are safe and secure in your own money.

Financial harmony is a sensation of having enough for essential requirements, desires, trip plans, family responsibilities, and much more. It's virtually hard to put an exact value on financial harmony. Some get it when they hit six figures, others probably don't get it until they are in the millions, or tens of millions. Identify what your number is and strive toward it.

The value of financial independence extends way beyond the cash amount or balance sheet. More options, greater relationships, a new attitude, less stress, more confidence–these are all advantages that go beyond the financial number.

Gaining control of personal money and ultimately reaching financial independence is a reflection of our beliefs, the way we live, the choices we make, and our capacity to follow through on plans. So it's not just about money–it's about all of these things–ultimately resulting in financial independence.

Setting the Stage for a Personal Financial Transformation

Putting the degree for a private financial transformation is corresponding to getting ready the canvas for a masterpiece. It calls for a conscious acknowledgment of your modern-day economic panorama, a mirrored image for your aspirations, and a dedication to fostering alternatives. This journey toward monetary freedom is not just about crunching numbers; it is about know-how the complex dance among your values, aspirations, and the assets at your disposal.

take into account this moment as the threshold of a brand new bankruptcy for your monetary tale. It starts with a deep dive into your current financial situation—an honest evaluation of your profits, costs, property, and liabilities. This self-attention lays the muse for the transformation that follows. it's now not about judgment but approximately expertise in which you stand so that you can chart a path forward.

As you survey the economic terrain of your existence, don't forget your goals. What are your quick-term and long-term aspirations? What dreams do you harbor for yourself and your loved ones? Your goals are the compass guiding your monetary decisions, and articulating them is a crucial part of this transformative procedure. They serve as the North superstar, providing direction and motive.

The canvas also includes your economic behavior and behaviors. Are they leading you toward prosperity or hindering your progress? figuring out patterns of spending, saving, and making an investment is essential. This introspection exhibits the habits that make a contribution to monetary achievement and people that are probably impeding your adventure.

Furthermore, placing the level involves acknowledging the role of mindset on your monetary lifestyles. How do you perceive money? Is it a supply of stress, or do you view it as a device for empowerment? Cultivating a fantastic money attitude is pivotal for the journey beforehand. it is approximately rewiring your mind and beliefs to foster a wholesome dating with money—one that serves your goals as opposed to hinders them.

on this preparatory segment, understand the importance of monetary desires. They act as milestones to your journey, supplying motivation and a roadmap for selection-making. Whether it is constructing an emergency fund, paying off debt, or saving for a home, each purpose contributes to the larger narrative of financial freedom.

ultimately, renowned that exchange is a constant associate in this journey. Flexibility and flexibility are virtues as you craft your financial Freedom Blueprint. As we delve deeper into the techniques and ideas that underpin financial freedom, keep in mind that this isn't just about economic transformation; it's approximately a holistic shift for your technique to existence and the possibilities it presents

Chapter 1: Understanding Your Current Financial Situation

Assessing Your Income and Expenses

Evaluating one's income and expenditures is an essential initial stride towards attaining agency over one's financial trajectory. Comparable to examining one's own financial well-being, it offers an unobstructed depiction of the present state of one's finances.

Throughout this procedure, your spending habits, financial capabilities, and the intricate link between them will all be carefully examined.

Understanding Your Income

Earnings is the lifeblood of your economic lifestyles, the gasoline that powers your aspirations and everyday life. start this assessment with the aid of taking a comprehensive inventory of all of your earnings sources. This includes your primary activity, side hustles, freelance paintings, and some other avenues from which cash flows into your lifestyles.

take into account now not the simplest quantity however also the consistency of your profits. Is it hard and fast profits, hourly wages, or irregular profits from various resources? know-how the predictability of your earnings is critical for developing a solid financial foundation.

Moreover, delve into the after-tax aspect of your profits. The cash you are taking domestically is what shapes your financial selections. analyze your tax deductions, and bear in mind any extra profits streams, together with bonuses, dividends, or presents. spotting the full spectrum of your earnings provides a sensible image of your monetary assets.

As soon as you have cataloged your income sources, compare the capacity for increase. Are there possibilities for income to increase, career advancements, or expanding your facet hustles? identifying avenues for growing your income sets the degree for a better financial future.

Understanding Your Expenses

On the opposite side of the financial equation are your expenses—the outflows that may either drive you toward your objectives or hamper your progress. Begin by separating your spending into fixed and variable costs. Fixed expenditures, like rent or mortgage payments, stay constant, whereas variable expenses, such as food and entertainment, vary.

Developing a precise summary of your month-to-month spending is a watch-establishing hobby. tune every greenback spent over a given time, classifying spending precisely. This method uncovers expenditure tendencies and shows locations where changes can be warranted.

don't forget to utilize budgeting tools or apps to ease this technique. They provide a complete attitude of your economic transactions, making it easy to discover patterns, set up barriers, and sooner or later adjust your spending. A price range isn't always speculated to be pro scripting; rather, it lets you manipulate sources deliberately.

Next, compare discretionary expenditures. These are the non-critical expenditures that, despite the fact that delightful, can be draining resources from more good sized monetary targets. It might be the day by day coffee run, impulsive purchases, or subscriptions that accrue over the years. spotting and reducing discretionary expenditure is an essential step in the direction of financial discipline.

Debt duties are every other key aspect of your expenditure evaluation. listing all exceptional bills, inclusive of credit cards, loans, and different monetary commitments. understand the hobby costs, minimal payments, and general awesome quantities. Tackling excessive-interest debt is commonly a priority in the direction of economic independence.

Now, examine the need and cost obtained from each price. Are there locations where you could lessen fees without affecting your satisfaction? It can require negotiating bills, gaining knowledge of extra cheap options, or just being careful of your spending conduct. This perception is a crucial thing in organizing monetary attention.

Creating a Sustainable Balance

Assessing your profits and costs isn't just about the numbers on a ledger; it is about finding a sustainable stability that aligns along with your monetary desires. if your prices constantly outweigh your profits, it's a purple flag signaling the need for changes. This can involve exploring new earnings streams, slicing discretionary spending, or renegotiating fixed prices.

Conversely, if you discover yourself with surplus income, it opens doors to multiplied debt compensation, improved savings, and strategic investments. expertise the balance between profits and fees empowers you to make knowledgeable choices about your financial future.

Moreover, this assessment is not a one-time undertaking; it's an ongoing method. life is dynamic, and your economic panorama evolves. often revisiting and recalibrating your profits and fee evaluation guarantees that you live on route closer to your economic goals.

Strategies for Improvement

Having reviewed your revenue and spending, the next stage is adopting methods for improvement. This might mean negotiating bills to achieve cheaper rates, investigating options for professional growth or other income sources, and adjusting your budget to line with your financial objectives.

Consider constructing an emergency fund as a financial safety net. This reserve may assist cushion unforeseen costs and prevent them from derailing your financial progress. Aim for a reserve that covers three to six months' worth of living expenditures.

Additionally, analyze your debt landscape. Develop a strategy for paying off high-interest bills strategically. This could entail the snowball strategy, concentrating on lesser debts first, or the avalanche method, handling higher-interest loans to reduce total interest payments.

Making an investment in your economic education is likewise an incredible tactic. expertise in the fundamentals of making an investment, tax making plans, and wealth creation empowers you with the information to make educated financial choices. discover tools, guides, and publications that enhance your financial literacy.

In the end, the appraisal of your earnings and spending is the cornerstone of financial empowerment. It establishes the framework for aware financial choice-making, paving the street for a future of prosperity and balance. As you start in this progressive course, take into account that each step ahead is a stride closer to the economic independence you aim to perform.

Creating a Net Worth Statement

Creating a net worth statement is a pivotal step in gaining a complete expertise of your monetary health. It serves as an image, capturing the entirety of your economic photo via detailing your property, liabilities, and in the end revealing your net worth — a key indicator of your standard financial well-being.

Understanding Net Worth: The Big Picture

Net worth is the distinction between your overall assets and general liabilities. Assets are everything you own that holds value, from cash and investments to real estate and personal possessions. Liabilities, on the other hand, encompass your debts and financial obligations, such as loans and credit card balances.

An effective net worth signifies that your belongings outweigh your liabilities, indicating monetary health and the capability for future economic increase. Conversely, a poor internet really indicates that your money owed surpasses your property, highlighting regions for development and strategic monetary planning.

Compiling Your Assets: Taking Stock of What You Own

Begin by cataloging all your assets. This includes cash in bank accounts, investments in stocks and bonds, real estate, retirement accounts, and valuable personal possessions such as vehicles or jewelry. Be thorough and accurate in your assessment, considering both liquid and non-liquid assets.

Assign each asset a monetary value. For cash and investments, use current market values. For real estate, consider appraisals or recent comparable sales. Vehicles and personal possessions can be valued based on fair market value, acknowledging that depreciation may impact their worth.

Assessing Liabilities: facing monetary obligations Head-On

Next, compile a listing of all your liabilities. This encompasses mortgages, car loans, scholar loans, credit card balances, and other terrific debts. consist of the overall amount owed for every legal responsibility, in addition to the hobby costs related to them.

In contrast to belongings, liabilities constitute debts, and it's essential to have clean information of the amazing balances and their impact on your typical economic scenario. This transparency permits you to increase a strategic plan for debt control and compensation.

Calculating net worth: The economic Equation

Once you have compiled your listing of belongings and liabilities, the calculation is easy: subtract your overall liabilities out of your total property. The following figure is your net worth.

net worth = total belongings - popular Liabilities

A high-quality internet worth shows that your assets exceed your liabilities, reflecting a wholesome financial position. A poor internet worth indicators that your money owed are greater than your assets, highlighting areas that can require interest and monetary planning.

Interpreting the results: What Your internet worth exhibits

Your net worth isn't always just a numerical fee; it's a powerful indicator of your monetary trajectory. here's the way to interpret extraordinary situations:

1. Fine net worth: A high-quality net worth indicates financial health and suggests that your property offers a cushion in opposition to your liabilities. it's an encouraging signal that you are constructing wealth and have the capability for destiny monetary growth.

2. Terrible: net worth A bad internet worth might also indicate monetary challenges, which includes excessive debt stages. However, it's essential to view this as a possibility for improvement. via identifying and addressing areas contributing to bad internet worth, you could broaden techniques for debt reduction and wealth building.

3. Growing net worth: Monitoring your net worth over the years presents insights into the effectiveness of your financial selections. A constant boom in the internet really indicates that you are making sound monetary choices, efficiently coping with debt, and constructing wealth.

4. Stagnant or reducing net worth: If your net worth stays stagnant or decreases, it is a signal to re-evaluate your financial techniques. This may involve exploring possibilities to boom earnings, lessen liabilities, or optimize your investment and savings strategies.

Utilizing Your net worth Strategically

Past filling in as a preview of your ongoing monetary position, your total assets turns into an essential device for monetary preparation. This is the way to use it:

1. Objective Setting: Based on your analysis of your net worth, set financial goals. Whether it's obligation decrease, constructing a backup stash, or contributing for the future, your total assets explanation gives a guide to setting practical and feasible goals.

2. Planning and Spending: Choosing your budget is easier when you know your net worth. It gives clearness on where your cash ought to be apportioned and focuses on spending in light of your monetary objectives.

3. Obligation Management: For those with a negative total assets, zeroing in on obligation decreases turns into a need. Your total assets proclamation features which obligations are influencing your generally speaking monetary wellbeing the most, permitting you to foster a designated obligation reimbursement procedure.

4. Speculation Strategies: A positive total assets opens ways to speculate. With an unmistakable comprehension of your monetary assets, you can settle on informed conclusions about distributing assets to ventures that line up with your gamble resilience and monetary objectives.

5. Monetary Check-Ins: It is beneficial to update your statement of net worth on a regular basis. It gives continuous bits of knowledge into your monetary advancement and permits you to adjust your methodologies in view of changes in pay, costs, or economic situations.

Making a total assets explanation isn't simply a practice in calculating; it's a primary move toward monetary strengthening. It gives lucidity, uncovered regions for development, and offers a substantial measurement for checking your monetary wellbeing over the long run. As you leave on this excursion of self-disclosure and monetary preparation, recall that your total assets explanation is certainly not a proper report; a unique instrument develops with your life and monetary choices. Make strategic use of it, make any necessary adjustments to it, and let it lead you toward a prosperous and secure financial future.

Analyzing Debt and Liabilities

Examining obligations and liabilities is a pivotal part of grasping your generally monetary wellbeing. Obligation, while frequently thought to be a typical piece of monetary life, can fundamentally affect your capacity to accomplish independence from the rat race. This cycle includes a profound plunge into the idea of your obligations, their terms, and the general weight they put on your monetary prosperity. By examining and dissecting your obligations, you gain knowledge into how to oversee and at last dispose of them, preparing for a safer monetary future.

Understanding the Kinds of Debt

Debts come in different structures, each with its own arrangement of suggestions for your monetary picture. Contracts, vehicle advances, understudy loans, Mastercard adjustments, and individual credits are normal sorts of debts that people might convey. Contracts regularly address a significant, long haul responsibility, while Mastercard debts might collect more rapidly because of exorbitant loan costs.

Surveying Financing costs and Terms

One of the basic parts of examining obligations is understanding the financing costs related to each kind. Loan fees altogether influence the general expense of getting and the time it takes to take care of the obligation. Exorbitant interest obligations, for example, charge cards, can rapidly collect, making it trying to break free from the pattern of obligation.

Also, audit the details of your credits. Might it be said that they are fixed-rate or variable-rate? Fixed-rate credits offer dependability as the financing cost stays consistent over the advance term, though factor rate advances can vary in light of economic situations, possibly affecting your regularly scheduled installments.

Focusing on Obligations for Repayment

Not all obligations are made equivalent, and examining them includes focusing on which ones to handle first. Exorbitant interest obligations, frequently connected with Mastercards, can be a huge channel on your monetary assets. Focusing on the reimbursement of these exorbitant premium obligations can set aside your cash over the long haul and assist your excursion toward independence from the rat race.

Consider utilizing obligation reimbursement systems like the snowball technique or the torrential slide strategy. The snowball technique includes taking care of the littlest obligations first, giving a mental lift as you dispose of individual obligations. The torrential slide strategy, then again, focuses on obligations with the most elevated loan costs, limiting the general interest paid over the long run.

Haggling with Creditors

Obligation investigation likewise includes surveying your capacity to haggle with lenders. Assuming you end up battling to meet regularly scheduled installments or confronting exorbitant loan costs, it merits investigating choices to reconsider terms. Loan bosses might bring down financing costs, broaden installment periods, or propose different courses of action to assist you with dealing with your obligation all the more successfully.

Starting a discussion with loan bosses exhibits monetary obligation and a guarantee to satisfy your commitments. Numerous loan bosses like to work with people who are proactive in tending to their monetary difficulties as opposed to defaulting on installments.

Keeping away from Normal Obligation Traps

Understanding your obligation scene additionally requires an attention to normal entanglements that can prompt collecting more obligations. Exorbitant interest payday credits, for instance, can trap people in a pattern of obligation that is trying to break. Likewise, depending on Visas to cover everyday costs without an unmistakable arrangement for reimbursement can prompt a mounting weight of exorbitant interest obligation.

To keep away from these snares, developing sound monetary habits is fundamental. This incorporates planning really, building a just-in-case account to deal with startling costs, and living inside your means. By avoiding normal obligation traps, you make a more steady monetary establishment.

Fostering an Obligation Reimbursement Plan

Equipped with an unmistakable comprehension of your obligations, financing costs, and reimbursement terms, the subsequent stage is to foster an obligation reimbursement plan. This plan ought to be custom fitted to your monetary circumstance, taking into account factors like pay, costs, and the earnestness of obligation reimbursement.

Begin by posting every one of your obligations, including the all out balance, loan fee, and least regularly scheduled installment. Designate a part of your spending plan to obligation reimbursement, zeroing in on the most noteworthy need obligations first. While making least installments on different obligations, assign any extra assets to speed up the reimbursement of exorbitant interest obligations.

Building a Rainy day account for Monetary Resilience

Investigating obligation likewise includes perceiving the significance of building a just-in-case account. A backup stash fills in as a monetary wellbeing net, assisting you with exploring unforeseen costs without turning to extra getting. It goes about as a support against the unanticipated difficulties that life might toss your direction.

Monetary counsels frequently prescribe saving three to a half year of everyday costs in a backup stash. This asset gives inward feeling of harmony and monetary flexibility, permitting you to climate surprising tempests without wrecking your advancement toward obligation decrease and independence from the rat race.

Looking for Proficient Guidance

In the event that your obligation circumstance feels overpowering or complex, looking for proficient direction can be a savvy choice. Monetary counselors and credit directing administrations can give customized exhortation custom-made to your particular conditions. They can assist you with investigating obligation combination choices, haggle with lenders, and make a reasonable arrangement for obligation reimbursement.

Tending to the Underlying drivers of Debt

Investigating obligation isn't just about the numbers; about understanding the basic variables might add to obligation gathering. Way of life decisions, startling costs, and changes in pay can all assume a part. By tending to the main drivers, you can foster procedures to forestall future obligations and develop a more feasible monetary way of life.

This could include reevaluating ways of managing money, investigating extra revenue sources, or making a more vigorous spending plan. It's a chance for self-reflection and a promise to pursue decisions that line up with your drawn out monetary objectives.

Observing Advancement and Observing Successes

As you carry out your obligation reimbursement plan, it's urgent to routinely screen your advancement. Set achievements and celebrate little triumphs en route. Following your accomplishments gives inspiration and supports the positive monetary propensities you're developing.

Moreover, consistently reconsider your obligation and liabilities as your monetary circumstance develops. Changes in pay, startling bonuses, or acclimations to costs can all affect your obligation reimbursement system. Adaptability and flexibility are key as you explore the way to independence from the rat race.

Laying out Monetary Objectives

Do you feel like you're making a solid attempt to make the ideal choices with your cash yet never appear to excel? Or on the other hand have you been working extremely hard, perhaps getting a side gig, yet you don't have a lot to show for it toward the month's end?

Certainly, things like expansion and downturns are genuine and can feel like immense detours to your monetary objectives. Yet, in any event, when the economy isn't going off the deep end, on the off chance that you put forth no objectives for your cash, you'll feel like you're wasting your time.

What Is a Monetary Objective?

A monetary objective is any arrangement you have for your cash. You can have transient monetary objectives (like setting aside $1,000) or long haul monetary objectives (like purchasing a house or contributing for retirement). It's smart to define objectives for each aspect of your life, yet having explicit monetary objectives implies you're focusing on what you deeply desire by wanting to set aside and spend cash for those things.

In any case, contingent upon your relationship with cash, attempting to conclude how to manage it can feel as overpowering as picking what to watch on Netflix or as energizing as arranging an excursion to Disneyland. There are such countless choices. In any case, you can't observe all the home makeover shows or ride every one of the rides immediately. You must single out, and I suggest handling your objectives in a request that will set you up for deep rooted achievement. Above all, we should discuss how you can get in the outlook of putting forth objectives.

- **Moves toward Laying out Monetary Objectives**

Heaps of things can impact the manner in which you put forth your monetary objectives, including your inspirations, values and dreams for what's in store. What's more, the manner in which your folks dealt with cash and, surprisingly, your own spending and reserve funds propensities (which are novel to you) likewise significantly affects how you handle cash. Objective arranging takes expectation and some mindfulness, so cut out chances to ponder your objectives. Track down a couple of moments to plunk down with some espresso or a glass of wine and prepare to dream — huge! When you have a rundown of objectives for your cash as a top priority, you're prepared to separate them into more modest, noteworthy stages. How it's done:

1. Make your objective explicit.

One explanation individuals don't hit their cash objectives is on the grounds that they're excessively unclear. You could say, "I need to be better with cash." However, how might that really affect you? Slender it down. Or on the other hand, "I need to update my vehicle sometime in the not so distant future." Alright, fun! Yet, what sort of vehicle do you need, and when would you like to get it?

Imagine a scenario where you chose rather to handle your obligation. That is a particular region of your cash to zero in on. Presently, we should discuss how to separate this objective much more.

2. Make your objective quantifiable.

OK, so you want to take care of your obligations. Presently it is the right time to pick a definite sum — what you can quantify to be aware of the off chance that you hit your objective or not.

While being totally obligation free ought to be your definitive objective, it's really smart to separate that objective into more modest lumps. Like that, you have a dream of where you're going before you begin.

Let's assume you have $30,000 of all our obligations. You'll need to begin by taking care of your littlest obligation, similar to a $15,000 understudy loan, first. That is the very thing that I mean by defining a quantifiable objective.

3. Give yourself a cutoff time.

Here's the way things are looking: It's really simple to put off your objectives when they aren't time-delicate. Quit saying you'll begin sometime in the future. You really want to give yourself a cutoff time and make it sensible — yet additionally somewhat testing.

Back to the understudy loan model: When would you like to hit your objective? To pay off $15,000 in one year, you'll have to pay $1,250 every month. Is this conceivable yet additionally somewhat of a stretch? Assuming this is the case, great!

Presently, a few objectives fall into the short-to mid-term classification, and these can be handled in under five or something like that. Consider long haul objectives ones you'll accomplish in five years or more.

Here are a few instances of short-and long haul monetary objectives:

Short-and mid-term monetary objectives:

- Setting aside a backup stash
- Putting something aside for a get-away
- Paying for books for an impending semester of school
- Purchasing another kitchen apparatus or redesign
- Putting something aside for a wedding band
- Putting down a store on a condo rent
- Putting something aside for impending clinical or dental administrations
- Purchasing birthday or Christmas presents
- Saving a house up front installment

Long haul monetary objectives:

- Purchasing another vehicle with cash
- Paying for your child's school in real money
- Putting something aside for retirement
- Sending off a business
- Going for a very long time

4. Ensure they're your own objectives.

At the point when we contrast ourselves with others, we're playing a game we won't ever win. Thus, ensure you're defining monetary objectives that seem OK for you. To put it another way, you shouldn't take out a second mortgage just because your friends are renovating their kitchens. Is that one Instagram force to be reckoned with taking another luxurious get-away? Hello, bravo. In any case, that doesn't mean you really want to do exactly the same thing — or that you're behind throughout everyday life on the off chance that you're not in a similar spot. Put the blinders on, center around your objectives, and focus on front and center. Furthermore, be sure about why you've picked the objectives you have.

5. Put down your objective.

Did you know you're bound to accomplish your objectives assuming you get them on paper? That's right, it's valid — something doesn't add up about putting pen to paper that assists you with focusing on the job needing to be done.

Thus, feel free to record your objectives. After that, adhere them to your desk, bathroom mirror, or car. You can make them the first thing you see when you pick up your phone by typing them into a notes app on your phone, taking a screenshot of them, and setting them as your wallpaper. Keeping your objectives where you can see them will keep you on target and inspired.

6. Find a buddy who will hold you accountable for achieving your goals.

To make your objectives one stride further, track down an objective responsibility mate. This could be your mate, a dear companion or a local area — any individual who will support you and check in as you continue dealing with hitting your objective. Having a team promoter in your corner and knowing you're in good company can have a colossal effect as you make progress toward your objectives.

Instances of Monetary Objectives

With such a lot of cash "counsel" drifting around, it tends to be difficult to tell which monetary objectives you ought to go for the gold. For this reason I need to specify the Child Steps when I discuss defining monetary objectives. The Child Steps will assist you with putting something aside for crises, take care of obligation, and create financial wellbeing. In any case, there's a cycle to follow.

Should you first eliminate debt? Save for your children's school? Purchase a home? Retirement investing? The 7 Gradual steps slice through all the disarray and give you a way to do everything. Following the means will assist you with zeroing in on each objective in turn so you can make more advancement with your cash and feel monetary harmony.

Assuming that you do not know what monetary objective to pursue first, begin by taking this speedy appraisal to figure out what Small step you're on.

Here are some of the most widely recognized monetary objectives individuals set and ways to get them going.

Are any of these on your rundown?

1. Make and adhere to a spending plan.

Not exclusively is planning one of the top monetary objectives individuals set each new year, but at the same time it's the establishment you ought to assemble all your other cash objectives on.

You can make progress with your money by sticking to a budget. It's an arrangement for what's coming in (your pay) and what's going out (your costs). You let your cash know where to go as opposed to pondering where it went. At the point when you have this arrangement for your cash, you can feel sure you're moving toward your objective consistently.

You can gain momentum in all areas of your finances by using a budget. Assuming you're as of now planning, bravo! On the off chance that not, get everything rolling free of charge with EveryDollar.

2. Develop a backup stash.

Life occurs. In any case, you can be ready for any cash issues that come your direction assuming you have sufficient cash set aside. I'm referring to issues with your vehicle, medical bills, and clogged toilets—all of which are unpleasant aspects of adulthood. However, if you have an emergency fund, you can rest assured that you won't have to borrow money to cover unexpected expenses.

Begin with the monetary objective of having $1,000 in reserve funds. Then, at that point, assuming you have an obligation, now is the right time to take that out. (I'll discuss that in a moment.) From that point forward, you need to develop a completely supported backup stash with 3-6 months of costs. (Again, all of this is covered in the Baby Steps, a tried-and-true strategy for controlling your finances.)

At the point when you have a rainy day account, you're prepared for those "life occurs" minutes. You won't have to worry about what might happen next because you'll know you've saved money to deal with it.

3. Reduce your debt.

Assuming you have an obligation, now is the right time to quit fooling around with taking care of it. Every last bit of it. Yeah, I know that may seem impossible right now, especially if you have a lot of big numbers—student loans, credit cards, or whatever else is in debt—in front of you. However, here's the undeniable reality: Obligation doesn't push you ahead. It keeps you down. You can't excel with your cash on the off chance that it's continuously going to moneylender installments.

4. Set something aside for your fantasy retirement.

We should require one moment to put on our creative mind covers and picture the best retirement. Perhaps that is five, 10 or 30 years not too far off. Would you like to get together with the grandchildren and go to Disney each Christmas? Visit another state with your companion once a quarter? Remain at home and read each book on your racks? Take up a great side interest or travel for global cooking illustrations?

Regardless of what you're dreaming for the future, you'll require great retirement ventures now to make it a reality. After you're without obligation and have a completely financed backup stash, I believe that you should begin money management 15% of your family pay for retirement. And what's more? When you have no debt, all of the money you spent on payments can be put directly into your accounts to help you save for your retirement.

5. Save more while spending less.

Lots of individuals whip objectives out of the air, similar to "I need to spend less" or "I need to save more," without pondering what it means to do those things as a matter of fact. Individuals, you must be explicit with your objectives and purposeful about your cash propensities.

Becoming fruitful with cash is more about changing your way of behaving than anything more. This could mean making a monthly budget and sticking to it, finding deals, using coupons, paying cash, or increasing your income. Also, a significant one: You must figure out how to say no — even to yourself. I'm not saying never have some good times. However, if you need to set aside cash, it will take some preparation and a way of life changing.

Lastly, here's one of my number one methods for spending less and saving more: Plan your feasts. Food is where most Americans overspend, and feast arranging is the way you reign that in. Find out how to save time and money on food by downloading my free Weekly Meal Planner and Grocery Savings Guide.

An Illustration of a Monetary Objective in action

Alright, so now that I've gone over the essentials of monetary objective preparation, let me provide you with an illustration of how this can function, in actuality.

Some time back, my better half, Lucy, and I chose to fabricate a house. Before that, all the additional pay we acquired went directly to our overall reserve funds. In any case, I knew building a house would cost a great deal, and irregular, unforeseen costs will undoubtedly spring up during the cycle. Thus, we made it an objective to set aside however much we could — explicitly toward our home. We gained so much momentum by breaking it down into monthly goals, even though saving that much money seemed almost impossible. Having an arrangement for our cash made our fantasy conceivable, however it likewise made the interaction fun.

Having this objective for our cash likewise kept my burning through propensities (otherwise known as spendencies — trust me, it's a thing) under control. Realizing my cash was going toward something I truly needed (far more than any late-night Amazon buys) persuaded me to spend less. What's more, despite the fact that there were minutes when we felt exhausted — I mean, there were a few days when all I needed to do was unwind and burn through cash — tracking down imaginative ways of hitting our objective quicker kept us on target every month.

Past that, it was character building. A period in our marriage we'll continuously think back on and realize we achieved something hard together. It contributed to the development of our connection and my own contentment. Now I know that the process's advantages are worth more than the new house.

Why is it important to set financial goals?

Having an objective assists you with being more future centered with your cash. You'll start to see how every choice affects your financial health as a whole and adds up.

For instance, on the off chance that you don't have monetary objectives, it's not a problem to purchase breakfast and espresso consistently. However, let's take a look at how much that actually costs you. You'll normally spend no less than $25 for only one full week of lattes — that is $100 per month! How else might you at any point manage that cash?

On the off chance that you put $100 in a venture account consistently for quite a long time, your latte asset could develop into more than $8,000, because of the force of compound development. That is an entire semester of your children's school you're drinking.

Suppose you thought much longer term and contributed $100 per month for a considerable length of time. Your latte investment funds could develop to more than $45,000.

Furthermore, on the off chance that you contribute your reserve funds for quite some time? Your espresso cash could develop to more than $280,000. A latte daily or a fourth of 1,000,000 bucks? You all, I like a decent mug of espresso — however not unreasonably much.

To get yourself in a position to be monetarily secure, see as little (or huge) penances you can make at the present time. The regular things you do with your cash today will totally influence your future.

Chapter 2: Budgeting for Success

The Significance of Planning

Planning is a fundamental mainstay of monetary prosperity, filling in as a guide for people and families to explore the complicated scene of pay and costs. At its center, planning is in excess of a simple practice in calculating; a useful asset enables people to assume command over their funds, pursue informed choices, and work towards accomplishing their monetary objectives.

Grasping Your Monetary Landscape

Planning gives a thorough preview of your monetary scene, offering lucidity and knowledge into the mind boggling snare of pay and costs. It permits you to see precisely where your cash is coming from and, all the more significantly, where it is going. This mindfulness is crucial to monetary education, empowering you to pursue informed decisions about your spending, saving, and financial planning.

Laying out Boundaries and Goals

One of the critical advantages of planning is its capacity to assist you with defining boundaries and monetary objectives. By apportioning explicit sums to various classifications like investment funds, obligation reimbursement, and optional spending, you guarantee that your cash lines up with your qualities and yearnings. Whether your objectives incorporate structure, a backup stash, buying a home, or subsidizing your youngsters' schooling, a spending plan fills in as a diagram for transforming dreams into unmistakable monetary goals.

Monetary Discipline and Control

Planning imparts monetary discipline, making a system for capable cash the board. It empowers cognizant dynamics about costs, deters imprudent spending, and advances careful utilization. With a spending plan set up, you are less inclined to succumb to normal monetary traps, like collecting exorbitant interest obligations or overspending on unnecessary things.

Besides, a spending plan gives a feeling of command over your monetary predetermination. As opposed to feeling overpowered or helpless before monetary conditions, you become the modeler of your monetary future. This feeling of control is engaging, encouraging trust in your capacity to deal with monetary difficulties and pursue decisions that line up with your drawn out prosperity.

Obligation The executives and Reduction

Planning assumes an urgent part under water and decreases. It permits you to focus on obligation reimbursement by dispensing explicit assets to handle exceptional equilibriums decisively. Whether utilizing the snowball strategy to take care of more modest obligations first or the torrential slide technique to target exorbitant interest obligations, a financial plan guarantees that a part of your pay is devoted to breaking free from the shackles of obligation.

Building a Crisis Fund

Life is eccentric, and unforeseen costs can emerge whenever. A very much created financial plan incorporates arrangements for building and keeping a secret stash. This monetary wellbeing net fills in as a support against unanticipated conditions, for example, health related crises, vehicle fixes, or employment shortfall. Without a backup stash, people might end up depending on Visas or credits to take care of surprising expenses, prompting a pattern of obligation. A spending plan helps you proactively get ready for the unforeseen, cultivating monetary strength.

Working with Saving and Investing

Planning isn't just about addressing prompt necessities; it is a device for creating financial momentum and getting your monetary future. By dispensing a piece of your pay to reserve funds and speculations, you make a pathway to long haul monetary achievement. Whether putting something aside for retirement, a kid's schooling, or other life objectives, a financial plan guarantees that you methodically put away assets to support and develop your abundance after some time.

Stress Decrease and Further developed Well-being

Monetary pressure is an inescapable worry for some people, influencing mental and profound prosperity. Planning, by giving an organized way to deal with overseeing funds, eases this pressure. It permits you to face monetary difficulties head-on, foster methodologies for development, and experience a feeling of command over your financial issues. The inward feeling of harmony that accompanies monetary strength decidedly impacts by and large prosperity, cultivating a better relationship with cash.

Upgraded Navigation and Monetary Literacy

Planning is an important instrument for upgrading monetary education and direction. It develops a comprehension of monetary standards, for example, the significance of saving, the effect of loan fees, and the results of obligation. Furnished with this information, people are better prepared to come to informed conclusions about their monetary future. Whether assessing speculation open doors, surveying the moderateness of significant buys, or exploring complex monetary circumstances, a financial plan fills in as a compass for savvy navigation.

Basically, planning is a comprehensive way to deal with monetary administration. It goes past the adjusting of pay and costs; a unique interaction adjusts to life's progressions and developing monetary objectives. By embracing planning as an essential part of monetary obligation, people engage themselves to shape an eventual fate of monetary strength, security, and, at last, opportunity.

Making a Practical Spending plan

Making a practical spending plan is a groundbreaking undertaking that engages people to assume command over their funds, adjust their spending to their needs, and work towards accomplishing their monetary objectives. It is more than just a spreadsheet of numbers; rather, a powerful device mirrors your qualities, goals, and the remarkable conditions of your monetary excursion. Fundamentally, a sensible spending plan is a guide directing you through the mind boggling scene of pay and costs, encouraging monetary discipline, and making ready for a safer and prosperous future.

- **Track your income and expenses**

Keeping track of your income and expenses for at least a month is the first step in creating a realistic budget. You can utilize a calculation sheet, an application, or a notepad to record how much cash you bring in and how much cash you spend on different classes, like lodging, food, transportation, diversion, and so on. This will assist you with seeing where your cash proceeds to distinguish your fixed and variable costs. Fixed costs are those that stay similar consistently, like lease, home loan, or protection. Variable costs are those that change contingent upon your use or conduct, like food, utilities, or feasting out

- **Put forth your monetary objectives**

The second move toward making a practical spending plan is to define your monetary objectives, both present moment and long haul. Momentary objectives are those that you need to accomplish in something like a year, for example, putting something aside for an excursion, taking care of a Visa obligation, or purchasing another machine. Long haul objectives are those that you need to accomplish in over a year, like putting something aside for retirement, purchasing a house, or beginning a business. Your financial objectives ought to be SMART: particular, measurable, doable, pertinent, and time-bound. You could, for instance, say, "I want to save $10,000 for a down payment on a house in two years," as opposed to "I want to save more money."

- **Create a spending plan**

The third step in creating a realistic budget is to create a spending plan that divides your income equally between your expenses and investments or savings. A well known technique to make a spending plan is the 50/30/20 rule, which recommends that you burn through half of your pay on your requirements, 30% on your needs, and 20% on your reserve funds or ventures. Be that as it may, you can change these rates as indicated by your own circumstance and inclinations. The key is to ensure that your spending plan covers your fixed and variable costs, as well as your monetary objectives.

- **Screen and change your spending plan**

The fourth move toward making a sensible financial plan is to consistently screen and change your spending plan. You ought to survey your financial plan something like once per month to check whether you are adhering to your spending plan and meeting your monetary objectives. You ought to likewise contrast your real pay and costs with your assessed ones, and recognize any holes or inconsistencies. Assuming you observe that you are spending more than you acquire, or that you are not saving enough for your objectives, you ought to change your financial plan likewise. You can do this by expanding your pay, lessening your costs, or focusing on your objectives

- **Use devices and assets**

The fifth move toward making a reasonable spending plan is to utilize devices and assets that can assist you with your planning interaction. There are numerous applications, sites, books, and digital broadcasts that can offer you tips, exhortation, and direction on the most proficient method to make and keep a practical financial plan. A few models are Mint, You Really want a Financial Plan, The Complete Cash Makeover, and The Dave Ramsey Show. You can likewise look for proficient assistance from a monetary organizer, an instructor, or a mentor in the event that you really want more customized or concentrated help.

- **Celebrate your progress and reward yourself**

for your accomplishments as the sixth and final step in creating a realistic budget. Planning can be testing and unpleasant, however it can likewise be fulfilling and fulfilling. You ought to recognize your endeavors and victories, and indulge yourself with something that makes you cheerful and roused. For instance, you could get yourself another book, watch a film, or have a decent dinner. However, ensure that your rewards do not derail your financial objectives and are within your budget. Keep in mind that developing a realistic budget is not a one-time event but rather an ongoing process that necessitates discipline, dedication, and adaptability.

Overseeing Variable and Fixed Costs

Fixed costs are the costs that you can conjecture with certainty since they don't change from one month to another or period to period. They will generally take up the biggest level of your financial plan since they are things like lease or home loan installments, vehicle installments and insurance payments. Variable costs, then again, are difficult to be aware of before you bring about them. You can assess them, however there is the likelihood that they will be higher or lower than what you expected. Models are food, gas and utilities. As these models show, albeit optional spending is in many cases a variable cost, variable costs can be necessities as well.

A monetary counsel can assist you with assembling a monetary arrangement for your future.

What Are Fixed Costs?

Commonplace fixed costs incorporate vehicle installments, home loan or lease installments, insurance payments and land charges. Normally, these costs won't be quickly different. On the plus side, they're not difficult to plan for in light of the fact that they by and large stay something similar and are paid consistently. A few fixed costs might be optional, similar to a rec center participation or web-based feature membership.

Albeit these bills are steady every month, you might in any case have the option to bring down their expenses. Assuming you're pursuing a month to month administration that you seldom use, there might be an elective arrangement with a lower cost. For instance, think about a less expensive rec center participation or an alternate web-based feature. Furthermore, look for elective vehicle protection, medical coverage, extra security and property holders or leaseholders protection intended to set aside more cash.

At the point when you bring down your proper costs, you naturally set aside more cash every month or payroll interval. That is on the grounds that proper costs will generally take up the biggest level of your financial plan. So when you bring down your proper costs, you bring down the level of your spending plan that is given to them. This is an incredible option in contrast to being economical with your other spending choices, like purchasing new garments or requesting takeout. The smidgen you save money on your proper costs can include quick.

For instance, assuming you burn through $1,100 rather than $1,185 each month on lease, the nature of your loft and neighborhood may not change a lot. In any case, that $85 each month will transform into $1,020 in one year. The most outstanding aspect? You just need to bring in that cash saving choice once to see the prize.

What Are Variable Costs?

One approach to portraying variable costs is that they address your everyday spending choices. Do you purchase traditional or natural produce? Do you get Starbucks or make espresso at home? Not all factor costs are optional costs, be that as it may.

Albeit variable expenses are regularly optional costs, some might be necessities. Purchasing gas for your vehicle every month is a variable cost, as are vehicle fixes and support. Shopping for food is likewise a variable cost. Your service bills may likewise be variable costs since they might change from one month to another. For instance, you could spend more on power in July than you do in December due to cooling.

Variable costs might be more earnestly to shrivel than fixed costs since they can influence your way of life. You might need to pick either making supper and getting take-out. Or on the other hand perhaps you really want to choose purchasing new garments or seeing that new film. Scaling back factor costs requires more everyday self discipline than scaling back fixed costs.

Step by step instructions to Budgeting for Variable and Fixed Costs

Large numbers of your variable costs might turn out to be genuinely unsurprising. In this way, on the off chance that you go through the earlier year's credit and charge card explanations, you might start to see an example. For instance, perhaps you get a hairstyle like clockwork. However, might you at some point extend a hairstyle to the most recent month and a half? That would save you approximately three hairstyles, which at, say, $40 a pop, is $120.

You can likewise utilize the previous year's information to gauge the amount you commonly spend on classifications of variable costs. For instance, you could have a regular food items class, a utilities classification and a movement costs classification. Then, perceive the amount you spent on these classifications during the earlier year and gap that number by 12. You can then save that sum every month for every variable cost. Assuming you need, you might open separate investment accounts for every variable cost class. This could assist you with obviously perceiving the amount you have left to spend on every classification consistently. It could likewise transform variable costs into costs you can expect and a spending plan for every month, very much like your proper costs.

Another normal planning tip incorporates checking fixed costs. Assuming your insurance payment will go up in the following year, you can design ahead of time for that. Drop any month to month benefits you didn't understand you were all the while paying for, as well. Keeping steady over month to month charges will assist you with ensuring you're not paying for anything you don't utilize.

Keep in mind, whether you're setting spending limits, focusing on costs, or essentially following your cash, the way to plan is to change depending on the situation. Thus, assuming that you are reliably overspending in one region, you might need to scale back or track down alternate ways of lessening spending. Notwithstanding, overseeing fixed and variable costs can assist you with arriving at your monetary objectives effectively.

Systems for Saving and Reducing Expenses

Setting aside cash and reducing expenses are fundamental parts of monetary prosperity. Key ways to deal with saving are not just assisting with building a rainy day account and accomplish momentary objectives yet in addition to long haul monetary security. How about we dive into explicit and viable techniques for saving and reducing expenses across different parts of the individual budget.

1. Automated Reserve funds: Set It and Fail to remember It

One strong procedure for saving is to mechanize the cycle. Set up for a piece of your pay to be consequently moved to a committed investment account every payday. This mechanized methodology kills the requirement for manual exchanges and guarantees predictable commitments to your reserve funds objectives. Whether it's for crises, future buys, or speculations, robotized investment funds make a trained and bother free method for building monetary stores

.

2. Budgeting with Accuracy: Track Each Dollar

Planning is a foundation of viable monetary administration. To reduce expenses and expand investment funds, foster a nitty gritty financial plan that tracks each dollar you procure and spend. Order your costs into fixed and variable, focus on needs over needs, and set sensible spending limits for optional things. Consistently audit and change your spending plan to reflect changes in pay, costs, and monetary objectives. This fastidious planning approach gives clearness and engages you to pursue purposeful spending choices.

3. Negotiating Bills: Trim Month to month Expenses

Lessening fixed costs can fundamentally influence your financial plan. Find opportunities to arrange bills like link, web, protection, and even utilities. Many specialist co-ops offer advancements or limits to hold clients. Research contenders' rates and influence this data during exchanges. Indeed, even an unassuming decrease in these proper expenses can prompt significant reserve funds after some time.

4. Meal Arranging and Cooking at Home: Adroit Staple Shopping

Food expenses frequently address a huge part of month to month financial plans. To reduce expenses, embrace feast arranging and cooking at home. Make a week by week feast plan, make a shopping rundown, and stick to it while shopping for food. Purchasing in mass, selecting nonexclusive brands, and using steadfastness projects can additionally decrease staple expenses. Furthermore, planning dinners at home sets aside cash as well as advances better dietary patterns.

5. Refinancing Obligation: Bringing down Interest Payments

On the off chance that you have extraordinary obligation, investigate amazing chances to renegotiate to bring down loan fees. This procedure is especially important for exorbitant interest obligations like Visas or specific sorts of advances. Renegotiating can prompt lower regularly scheduled installments, diminished by large interest installments, and facilitated obligation reimbursement. Be that as it may, cautiously survey the terms and any related charges prior to chasing after renegotiating choices.

6. Energy Proficiency: Trim Utility Bills

Executing energy-proficient practices at home can add to massive expense reserve funds. Basic activities like utilizing energy-effective lights, turning off electronic gadgets when not being used, and appropriately protecting your home can diminish power bills. Furthermore, consider moving up to energy-proficient apparatuses, which might fit the bill for discounts or expense impetuses, giving both present moment and long haul monetary advantages.

7. Subscription Reviewing: Smoothing out Diversion Costs

Survey and review your memberships consistently. Web-based features, magazine memberships, and other repeating costs can gather without notice. Assess whether every membership lines up with your ongoing advantages and way of life. In the event that not, consider dropping or downsizing plans to additional savvy choices. This cycle reduces superfluous expenses as well as guarantees that your amusement costs are deliberate and inside spending plan.

8. Bulk Buys and Limits: Amplifying Value

For specific things, mass buys and looking for limits can prompt significant investment funds. Think about purchasing durable things, cleaning supplies, or toiletries in mass to exploit lower unit costs. Moreover, effectively search for limits, use coupons, and investigate cashback or rewards programs while making buys. Being key about when and where you shop adds to predictable expense reserve funds after some time.

9. Emergency Asset as an Expense Mitigator: Forestalling Monetary Setbacks

While building a backup stash is basically a reserve funds procedure, it assumes a critical part in cost relief. A sufficiently supported secret stash goes about as a monetary cradle, keeping surprising costs from wrecking your spending plan. Mean to save three to a half year of everyday costs in your backup stash to shield against unanticipated conditions, for example, health related crises or unexpected vehicle fixes.

10. Financial Training and Do-It-Yourself Approach: Enabling Monetary Independence

Concentrating on monetary schooling can be a financially savvy procedure over the long haul. Finding out about individual budget, speculation standards, and essential Do-It-Yourself abilities can engage you to deal with assignments that could some way or another cause proficient expenses. Whether it's overseeing speculations, leading home fixes, or getting ready straightforward expense forms, a Do-It-Yourself approach adds to independence and decreases the requirement for outside administrations.

Key saving and cost-cutting include a multi-layered approach that tends to different parts of the individual budget. By integrating these definite methodologies into your monetary daily schedule, you can fabricate a vigorous investment funds establishment, cut superfluous expenses, and work towards accomplishing both present moment and long haul monetary objectives. Keep in mind, the critical lies in consistency, discipline, and adjusting these procedures to suit your special monetary conditions.

Chapter 3: Building a Solid Emergency Fund

The role of a Just-in-case account

A just-in-case account is basically cash that has been saved to cover life's startling occasions. The cash will permit you to live for a couple of months. Would it be a good idea for you to end up losing your employment or pay for something surprising that surfaces without straying into the red.
Consider it an insurance contract. Instead of paying charges to an organization, you're paying yourself cash that you can use sometime in the not too distant future. The money can be gotten rapidly and effectively assuming that some sad occasion ends up happening.

Here are key perspectives that feature the significant role of a secret stash:

1. Monetary Pad In the midst of Emergency:
Unanticipated Costs: Life is intrinsically capricious, and unforeseen costs can emerge without warning. Whether it's a health related crisis, vehicle fix, or unexpected employment misfortune, a secret stash goes about as a pad, permitting people to explore these emergencies without wrecking their monetary solidness.

2. Evasion of Exorbitant Interest Obligation:

Quick Admittance to Assets: Having a rainy day account implies you don't need to depend on Visas or credits to cover abrupt costs. This forestalls the aggregation of exorbitant interest obligation, which can be monetarily difficult over the long haul.

3. Steadiness During Employment Cutback or Pay Decrease:

Employment Cutback or Pay Decrease: A secret stash gives monetary dependability during times of employment cutback or huge pay decrease. It covers important everyday costs, like lease or home loan installments, utilities, and food, until elective types of revenue can be gotten.

4. Inward feeling of harmony and Diminished Monetary Pressure:

Inward feeling of harmony: Realizing that you have a monetary wellbeing net brings true serenity. The mental effect of having a monetary pad is huge, decreasing pressure and nervousness related to surprising monetary difficulties.

5. Anticipation of Resource Liquidation:

Safeguarding of Speculations: Without a just-in-case account, people might be compelled to exchange ventures or offer significant resources to meet prompt monetary necessities. A secret stash helps safeguard long haul ventures, permitting them to keep developing over the long haul.

6. Adaptability for Life Changes:

Life Advances: Life changes, for example, movement, vocation changes, or startling family occasions, frequently accompany related costs. A rainy day account gives the adaptability to explore these advances without endangering monetary prosperity.

7. Support for Wellbeing Related Costs:

Wellbeing Related Expenses: Wellbeing crises or unforeseen clinical costs can strain funds. A backup stash guarantees that fundamental doctor's visit expenses can be covered immediately, cultivating actual prosperity without compromising monetary wellbeing.

8. Scaffold to Protection Guarantee Payouts:

Protection Guarantee Deferrals: in case of protection claims, delays in payouts can happen. A backup stash goes about as a scaffold, taking care of prompt expenses until protection claims are handled and reserves are gotten.

9. Assistance of Independent direction:

Key Navigation: Having a just-in-case account works with key decision-production during monetary difficulties. It gives the space to breathe to assess choices, haggle with leaders, and pursue insightful decisions that line up with long haul monetary objectives.

10. Groundwork for Financial Slumps:

Financial Vulnerability: Monetary slumps and downturns can influence professional stability and pay dependability. A just-in-case account positions people to climate monetary vulnerabilities without undermining their monetary honesty.

11. Consolation of Monetary Obligation:

Development of Monetary Discipline: Keeping a backup stash empowers monetary obligation and discipline. It is a proactive step towards building a strong monetary establishment and imparts propensities for putting something aside for the unforeseen.

12. Long haul Monetary Flexibility:

In general Monetary Flexibility: A secret stash adds to long haul monetary versatility. It goes about as a basic structure block for accomplishing more extensive monetary objectives, like homeownership, instruction, and retirement, by safeguarding people from difficulties that could somehow obstruct progress.

A backup stash assumes an imperative part in safeguarding people and families from monetary shocks, giving a feeling that everything is good, and empowering them to explore life's vulnerabilities with certainty and flexibility. Laying out and reliably adding to a secret stash is a principal part of sound monetary preparation and a vital stage towards accomplishing in general monetary prosperity.

Deciding the Perfect Sum for Your Fund

How much emergency savings you want relies upon your own monetary circumstance, including your pay, your costs and the requirements of your wards. There are a few common guidelines of thumb you can apply to think of a savings objective that works for you.

To begin with, numerous specialists prescribe saving sufficient cash to cover three to a half year of fundamental everyday costs. That is just the fundamentals: lease or home loan installments, bills, essential food, youngster care and such.

However, you could decide to save more than that in certain conditions. For instance, in the event that you're a consultant, project worker or somebody whose pay shifts from one month to another, you could point higher. The equivalent could be valid on the off chance that you're the sole worker for various wards.

Yet, on the off chance that saving several months of fundamental costs sounds overpowering, begin with a savings objective that works for you. Meaning to put $1,000 or even $500 in emergency savings can be major areas of strength for an off point.

Here are key contemplations to assist you with deciding the perfect sum for your emergency reserve:

1. Monthly Living Expenses:

Compute Necessities: Start by working out your fundamental month to month everyday costs. This incorporates expenses like lease or home loan installments, utilities, food, protection, and other fundamental bills.

Consider Lifestyle: Change the estimation in light of your way of life and ways of managing money. Assuming there are optional costs that you think are fundamental, remember them for your evaluation.

2. Job Dependability and Pay Sources:

Survey Occupation Stability: Assess the dependability of your work or pay sources. People with more steady work might incline towards a marginally more modest emergency reserve, while those with variable pay or occupation vulnerability might select a bigger pad.

Variable Pay Considerations: Assuming you have variable pay, consider assessing the sum expected to cover everyday costs during lean months.

3. Risk Resistance and Solace Level:

Assess Chance Tolerance: Evaluate your own gambling resilience. On the off chance that you have a higher gamble resistance and trust in your capacity to get elective pay rapidly, you could incline towards a more modest emergency reserve.

Solace Level: Consider your solace level with monetary vulnerability. A few people favor a bigger emergency asset to give a more prominent feeling of safety and genuine serenity.

4. Health Protection and Family Considerations:

Health care coverage Coverage: Assess your health care coverage inclusion. In the event that you have extensive health care coverage, you might require a more modest emergency store for possible clinical costs. On the other hand, restricted or no health care coverage could warrant a bigger asset.

Family Obligations: Think about family commitments. On the off chance that you have wards or extra monetary obligations, a bigger emergency asset might be judicious to represent unexpected blood related costs.

5. Job Market and Industry Factors:

Industry Volatility: Evaluate the instability of your industry or occupation market. People in unstable ventures might focus on a bigger emergency asset to explore possible cutbacks or industry slumps.

Market Conditions: Think about more extensive financial circumstances. During times of financial vulnerability or downturn, people might decide on a bigger emergency reserve.

6. Short-Term and Long haul Goals:

Assess Goals: Think about your present moment and long haul monetary objectives. Assuming you have explicit objectives, for example, homeownership or beginning a business, that might require critical monetary responsibilities, factor these into your emergency reserve estimation.

Separate Savings Goals: Recognize your emergency reserve and different savings objectives to try not to exhaust the emergency store for non-crises.

7. Insurance Inclusion and Deductibles:

Survey Insurance Policies: Assess the inclusion and deductibles of your protection contracts. Assuming you have far reaching inclusion with sensible deductibles, this might affect the sum you assign to your emergency store.

Emergency Asset as Deductible Reserve: Consider treating your emergency store as a deductible save for protection claims.

8. Consideration of Nearby Expense of Living:

Figure Neighborhood Costs: Consider the average cost for many everyday items in your topographical region. Greater expense regions might warrant a bigger emergency asset to cover fundamental costs.

9. Review and Change Regularly:

Customary Reviews: Occasionally survey and change your emergency store in light of changes in your day to day existence conditions, pay, and monetary objectives.

Life Events: Significant life altering situations, like marriage, having kids, or purchasing a home, may require changes in accordance with your emergency reserve.

10. Financial Counsels and Expert Guidance:

Look for Proficient Advice: If questionable, look for guidance from monetary counselors. Experts can give customized direction in light of your special circumstance, assisting you with deciding a proper emergency store sum.

Deciding the perfect sum for your emergency fund requires a far reaching evaluation of your monetary scene and individual contemplations. It's a harmony between giving an adequate wellbeing net to unexpected conditions and guaranteeing that your cash is effectively pursuing your more extensive monetary objectives. Customary surveys and changes, alongside thought of different elements, will assist you with keeping a very much adjusted emergency reserve that lines up with your monetary requirements and desires.

Where to Keep Your Emergency Fund

Choosing the right location for your emergency fund involves balancing accessibility, safety, and potential returns. The primary goal is to ensure that your funds are readily available when needed, while also considering factors like liquidity and the opportunity for modest growth.

1. Savings Account:

Accessibility: Savings accounts are highly accessible, allowing you to withdraw funds whenever needed. Many financial institutions provide online and mobile banking, making it easy to manage your emergency fund.

Safety: Funds in savings accounts are typically insured by government agencies up to a certain limit, providing a high level of safety. For example, in the United States, the Federal Deposit Insurance Corporation (FDIC) insures deposits up to $250,000 per depositor.

Liquidity: Savings accounts offer liquidity, enabling quick access to funds without penalties or restrictions. However, interest rates on savings accounts may be lower compared to other options.

2. Money Market Account:

Higher Interest Rates: Money market accounts often offer slightly higher interest rates compared to regular savings accounts. While the difference may be modest, it provides some opportunity for your emergency fund to grow.

Accessibility: Money market accounts provide easy access to funds through checks, debit cards, or online transfers. Like savings accounts, they are subject to federal insurance limits.

3. Certificates of Deposit (CDs):

Higher Interest Rates with Fixed Terms: Certificates of Deposit (CDs) typically offer higher interest rates than savings accounts or money market accounts. However, CDs come with fixed terms, ranging from a few months to several years.

Penalties for Early Withdrawal: While CDs offer higher interest, there may be penalties for withdrawing funds before the maturity date. Consider the trade-off between higher interest rates and the flexibility of access when choosing CDs for your emergency fund.

4. Online Banks:

Competitive Interest Rates: Online banks often offer higher interest rates on savings and money market accounts compared to traditional brick-and-mortar banks. This can potentially enhance the growth of your emergency fund.

Accessible: Online banks provide convenient access to funds through online platforms and mobile apps. Confirm that the online bank is FDIC-insured or insured by an equivalent agency.

5. Credit Union Accounts:

Member-Owned: Credit unions are member-owned financial institutions that may offer competitive interest rates on savings and money market accounts.

Access and Services: Credit unions often provide personalized services and may have fewer fees compared to larger banks. Confirm that the credit union is insured by the National Credit Union Administration (NCUA) or an equivalent agency.

6. Treasury Securities (T-Bills):

Government-Backed Security: Treasury bills (T-Bills) are short-term government securities that are considered very safe. They are upheld by the United States government.

Fixed Terms and Competitive Rates: T-Bills have fixed terms (e.g., 4 weeks, 13 weeks) and competitive interest rates. However, they are not as liquid as savings or money market accounts, and you may need to sell them on the secondary market before maturity.

7. Roth IRA (as a Last Resort):

Tax Advantages: While not typically recommended due to potential tax implications and penalties, a Roth IRA could serve as a last resort for emergency funds. Contributions (not earnings) can be withdrawn penalty-free, providing a source of funds in dire circumstances.

Long-Term Investment: A Roth IRA is primarily designed for retirement savings, and using it as an emergency fund should be considered only after exploring more conventional options.

Important Considerations:

Emergency Fund Size: The size of your emergency fund may influence your choice. If your fund is relatively small, easy accessibility might take precedence. For larger funds, considering options with higher interest rates may be more attractive.

Inflation Considerations: While safety and accessibility are crucial, it's important to consider the impact of inflation. Striking a balance between safety and the potential for modest growth helps preserve the purchasing power of your emergency fund over time.

Where you keep your emergency fund depends on your financial goals, risk tolerance, and the need for accessibility. A common approach is to use a combination of options, such as a savings account for immediate needs and a combination of CDs or higher-yield accounts for longer-term reserves. Regularly reassess your financial situation and explore opportunities to optimize the safety and growth potential of your emergency fund.

Handling Unexpected Expenses

Managing unexpected expenses can lose your budget track and cause pressure. Notwithstanding, with a few adaptability and brilliant methodologies, you can explore even the most badly designed monetary shocks. This is the way to actually deal with unexpected expenses:

These procedures can assist you with finishing what has been started when you need to dunk into your rainy day account or cash set to the side for unexpected expenses or occasions.

We as a whole have our month to month charges: lease, utilities, protection, vehicle installment or understudy loans. We as a whole purchase food and every so often eat out. These are the ordinary expenses we have all generally expected, and we as a whole arrangement our budgets around them.

Be that as it may, we don't necessarily make arrangements for the minutes when the suppressor tumbles off the vehicle or a mishap lands you in the trauma center. As per a study, just 39% of individuals would have the option to take care of a $1,000 unexpected bill from their investment funds. Whether you have an unexpected cost you really want to pay today or you're simply kicking a secret stash off, here are a few plans to consider while putting something aside for unexpected expenses.

Work with charge card organizations when an unexpected occasion happens

Americans have a typical charge card surplus of $5,221, which can bring about installments that remove enormous lumps from your check. The weight of these installments can develop as interest constructs, particularly on the off chance that you are behind for a little while.

There are possibilities for working with your Mastercard bank to diminish your responsibility, and many organizations will be glad to examine your choices. You can request that they eradicate past late expenses, or even arrange a decreased regularly scheduled installment that is more lined up with your check. A portion of these choices might influence your credit or credit lines, so make certain to investigate your choices.

Offer your stuff to let loose cash for unexpected expenses

Gone are the times of yard deals for making a fast payday. Nowadays, you can go to web based business sites to sell your unnecessary effects. You can place last year's closet available to be purchased up for sale destinations, and bring in cash selling your specialty on locales like Etsy and Ebay. You might try and have the option to sell a few things by means of neighborhood-explicit applications like Nextdoor.

Acquire additional pay to put something aside for unexpected expenses

On the off chance that you work a run of the mill everyday work, making the most of your extra energy around evening time and toward the end of the week can assist with developing extra reserve funds to take care of an unexpected cost rapidly. Think about customary positions — retail, client care or the food business — yet additionally contemplate taking on more modest tasks, for example, partaking in web based advertising research or virtual paid center gatherings.

Take on a momentary individual credit

Taking on a transient individual credit from your bank can assist with facilitating the one-time cost of an unexpected cost. Think about little credits — $100 to $1,000 — that you will actually want to repay inside a sensible measure of time. These credits will permit you to spread the expenses of a cost over various months, rather than compelling you to pay the sum forthright. Survey the details of any credit arrangement cautiously, particularly the charges and loan fees you could be paying - some of which could be huge, contingent upon the moneylender.

Re-budget to live underneath your means

There are a few expenses that you can't stay away from — lodging, transportation and food — yet you can think about scaling back unnecessary spending. The typical American burns through $2,913 on diversion every year. While it is essential to have fun occasionally, scaling back a couple of evenings out or dropping one of your web-based video real time features will appear in your financial balance.

Request a check advance to cover unexpected expenses

Contingent upon your manager, you might have the option to get compensated ahead of time for work you will do before very long. All organizations are unique, and you ought to chat with your chief, supervisor or an individual from HR about the particular organization rules.

Ensure you're ready for next time by saving at this point

Anything your unexpected cost, at least one of these systems will basically assist with getting it paid off. Consider setting aside cash for unexpected expenses in a high return reserve funds or currency market account proceeding — having even a modest quantity saved in a backup stash will help you with regards to the weight of your next unexpected cost.

Chapter 4: Debt Management Strategies

Debt management alludes to the most common way of coordinating and controlling debt in a manner that limits monetary gamble and boosts the capacity to meet monetary objectives.

It includes surveying one's debt circumstance, making an arrangement to reimburse debts, and executing procedures to forestall future debt-related issues.

Debt management is significant for people who have assumed advances, Mastercard debt, or different types of debt, as well with respect to organizations that depend on getting back their tasks.

Significance of Successful Debt Management

Successful debt management is fundamental for keeping up with monetary steadiness and forestalling the unfortunate results of over the top debt, for example, liquidation, harmed financial assessments, and expanded feelings of anxiety.

By effectively overseeing debt, people and associations can work on their monetary wellbeing, get a good deal on interest installments, and accomplish long haul monetary objectives.

Debt Management Plans (DMPs)

Debt management plans are formal arrangements among borrowers and credit guiding organizations that solidify uncollateralized debts into a solitary regularly scheduled installment.

DMPs can assist people with decreasing loan costs, postpone charges, and lay out an organized reimbursement plan, making it simpler to oversee and in the long run dispose of debt.

Debt Combination

Debt solidification includes consolidating different debts into a solitary credit with additional great terms, for example, lower loan fees or longer reimbursement periods. This debt management methodology improves on reimbursement and can get a good deal on interest installments over the long run.

Debt Repayment

Debt repayment is a debt management technique where borrowers haggle with leaders to acknowledge a lower installment than everything owed, successfully paying off the all out debt.

This choice can give alleviation for borrowers critical debt without collateral, yet it might adversely influence FICO ratings and ought to be thought about cautiously.

Bankruptcy

Bankruptcy is a lawful interaction that permits people or organizations to release or rearrange their debts under court watch.

While bankruptcy can give a new beginning to those overpowered by debt, it has durable ramifications for FICO ratings and ought to just be sought after if all else fails in debt management.

Snowball versus Torrential slide Strategies

The snowball and torrential slide techniques are two famous debt management systems for reimbursing different debts. The snowball technique focuses on taking care of debts with the littlest equilibriums first, while the torrential slide strategy targets debts with the most elevated financing costs.

The two strategies can be suitable in debt management, and the choice depends upon individual tendencies and financial conditions.

Types of Debt

Individual Debt Management
- **Visa Debt**

Credit Card debt is a typical type of unstable advance that emerges when people spend more on their charge cards than they can stand to take care of every month.

Successful debt management techniques for Visa debit incorporate paying more than the base installment, arranging lower loan fees, and merging exorbitant interest adjusts.

- **Understudy Loan Debt**

Understudy loan debt is caused when people get cash to fund their schooling. Debt management strategies for educational loans can incorporate pay driven reimbursement plans, advance absolution programs, and renegotiating to get lower financing costs.

- **Contract Debt**

Contract debt alludes to credits taken out to buy a home or property. Debt management for home loans might include renegotiating to get lower financing costs, making additional installments to lessen chief equilibrium, or using government help programs for property holders.

- **Car Credit Debt**

Car credit debt is made when people finance the acquisition of a vehicle. Dealing with this kind of debt can include renegotiating for better terms, taking care of the credit early, or exchanging the vehicle for a more reasonable choice.

Corporate Debt Management

- **Bank Credits**

Bank credits are a type of corporate debt that organizations use to back tasks or extensions. Debt management systems for bank advances incorporate haggling better terms with moneylenders, uniting various credits, and focusing on reimbursement to diminish generally speaking revenue costs.

- **Bonds**

Bonds are debt protections given by organizations to raise capital. Corporate debt management for securities can include renegotiating at lower financing costs, repurchasing extraordinary securities, or decisively giving new securities to oversee exceptional debt.

Business Paper

Business paper is a present moment, an unstable corporate debt instrument ordinarily given to meet transient funding needs.

Compelling debt management for business paper might incorporate renegotiating with longer-term debt, laying out credit extensions, or using different wellsprings of working capital.

Government Debt Management

- **Sovereign Debt**

Sovereign debt is given by public legislatures to back open spending and address monetary issues. Debt management for sovereign debt can include rebuilding reimbursement terms, arranging loan costs, or carrying out financial approaches to diminish shortfalls.

- **Metropolitan Bonds**

Metropolitan bonds are debt protections given by nearby state run administrations to back open tasks. Debt management for metropolitan securities can incorporate renegotiating existing securities at lower loan fees, carrying out income producing strategies, or focusing on reimbursement of exorbitant interest debt.

Prioritizing and Paying Off Debt

Having numerous debts is overpowering for the vast majority, which makes them search for ways of paying off the debts as fast as could really be expected. The strategy to dispose of debts for the most part includes repaying debts individually.

The issue with depts is dependably their intensifying viewpoint that open debts produce the more they are dynamic. This occurs because of its interest rate fixing. Notwithstanding, every monetary circumstance is remarkable and requires individual perception and strategy.

Which debt ought to be taken care of first relies upon the borrowers' monetary capacities, costs, pay, and other monetary commitments they have. Then again, certain universals can be applied in distinguishing the debt that ought to be focused on to pay off.

Prioritizing a Debt with The Most noteworthy Loan cost

Debts with the highest interest rate are the ones that cost you the most cash. Despite the fact that these debts probably won't be the ones with the highest chief sum, over the long haul, the ones with the highest interest are the most costly debts, while proceeding to pay the base installments of your different debts.
Thus, paying off the debt that has the highest interest rate will set aside the most cash and diminish the all out cost over the long run.

Subsequent to paying off your most costly debt, you can continue with this strategy to your second-highest-rate debt and proceed with the example until you take care of every one of your debts.

The debts with the highest interest rate are often Visas and individual advances. Optional rates with high interest are long haul rates, for example, understudy loans and home value credit extensions and some vehicle advances. The most reduced interest rates ordinarily consider the debts with the longest reimbursement terms, for example, contract advances and some business credits.

The technique for prioritizing paying off the debts with the highest interest rate is additionally called torrential slide debt reimbursement.

Prioritizing a Debt with The Littlest Equilibrium

In spite of the torrential slide debt reimbursement technique, there is a debt snowball strategy. On something contrary to prioritizing paying off the debt with the highest interest rate, this technique centers around paying the base regularly scheduled installments to all debts, however , guiding the additional cash to kill the debts with the littlest equilibrium first.

In the wake of repaying the principal debt, take the month to month cash sum and go along with it in the second littlest equilibrium least regularly scheduled installment, going on with this training with every one of your debts.

Making the biggest installments on the following littlest debt makes the debt compounding phenomenon. With this strategy, you can see the outcomes all the more rapidly.

This strategy is centered around inspiration and energy. Repaying the littlest equilibrium initially is the reasonable answer for individuals that miss the mark on inspiration and discipline to remain on a course that the torrential slide debt reimbursement strategy requires.

Prioritizing the Biggest Equilibrium Debt

Prioritizing the biggest equilibrium debt is certainly not a well known technique to begin taking out your debts. Notwithstanding, now and again, this can be the best beginning stage in liberating yourself of debts.

Some biggest equilibrium debts can be considered as need, for example,

Assuming your biggest equilibrium is in the 0% interest rate special period and you need to reimburse it before that period closes

In the event that piece of the equilibrium has a higher APR because of specific exchange types

Assuming that the biggest equilibrium is hurting your FICO rating (assuming you are utilizing over 30% of the accessible credit limit)

Paying off the biggest equilibrium debt strategy typically considers ultimately changing to accelerate or torrential slide practice after the biggest equilibrium debt is reimbursed.

Debt Combination

Debt combination can be the ideal choice in conditions when you are not fit for paying off your equilibrium in the following five years or when every one of your debts have such a high-interest rate which makes it unthinkable for you to reimburse them rapidly and soon. These can be the justifications for why debt solidification is the suitable arrangement.

Debt solidification considers getting new funding that will take care of all your ongoing debts.

In the event that the vast majority of your current debts are Visa debts, you can combine those debts by utilizing a Mastercard balance move.

Then again, on the off chance that your debts are other than charge cards and surpass how much 5.000$, the arrangement may be a debt solidification credit.

As referenced, debt combination suggests paying off the entirety of your debt adjusts on the double.
The upside of debt solidification is in limiting interest charges applied to your past debts. This way you can take care of the debt standards quicker.

Focus on the Debt with The Highest APR

This technique is viewed as cost-saving. APR is a yearly advance expense. The contrast between interest rate and APR is that the second incorporates different charges and extra expenses, for example, credit beginning charges, contract protection, shutting expenses, and others. APR is demonstrated in rates very much like an interest rate.

Debts with APR will quite often set you back more cash every month in light of the fact that every month that you leave your offset with APR applied you need to pay for it. Thus, most monetary specialists suggest paying off debts with APR first, as they squander your cash the most.

This sort of debt payoff prioritizing is otherwise called the torrential slide technique, as it additionally gives speedy speed increase.

Other than the referenced standards for prioritizing debt reimbursement, there are a few debts that probably won't be basically as costly as others yet are causing us more monetary and close to home pressure. These debts probably won't have anything alluding to the high-interest rates or adjust yet have an individual importance.

Haggling With Lenders

Haggling with lenders is a basic expertise while confronting financial difficulties. Whether managing Mastercard organizations, moneylenders, or different loan bosses, compelling exchange can prompt better terms and possibly mitigate financial strain. The following are five central issues to consider while haggling with loan bosses, each examined exhaustively:

1. Grasping Your Financial Situation:

Haggling with lenders starts with your very own careful comprehension of financial circumstances. Prior to starting any conversations, assess your pay, costs, and generally obligation commitments. Make a definite spending plan that obviously frames your financial standing, including your capacity to make installments.

Begin by ordering a rundown of every one of your obligations, noticing loan fees, exceptional equilibriums, and the sort of obligation. Evaluate your revenue sources and distinguish any progressions that might have happened, like an employment misfortune or decrease in pay. Moreover, analyze your financial plan to decide the most extreme sum you can practically allot towards obligation reimbursement without imperiling fundamental everyday costs.

While arranging, being furnished with an extensive comprehension of your financial position empowers you to introduce an unmistakable picture to banks. It additionally positions you to make sensible recommendations and set attainable reimbursement terms.

2. Open and Straightforward Communication:
Compelling correspondence is the foundation of effective discussions with banks. Move toward the exchange interaction with genuineness and straightforwardness. In the event that you're confronting financial troubles, don't avoid examining the difficulties you're encountering. Banks are much of the time more able to work with people who exhibit a genuine obligation to settling their financial commitments.

Start contact with lenders when you expect or encounter trouble making installments. Holding on until you're essentially behind on installments might restrict your arranging influence. Make sense of any conditions that have prompted your financial difficulties, like employment misfortune, clinical costs, or other unforeseen difficulties.

Obviously lucid your eagerness to meet your commitments and propose a practical arrangement for doing as such. Showing a proactive and informative methodology can encourage generosity and improve the probability of tracking down commonly pleasant arrangements.

3. Proposition for Updated Terms:
While haggling with banks, it's vital to come ready with a thoroughly examined proposition for overhauled terms. Banks are bound to think about elective game plans on the off chance that you can show a doable arrangement for reimbursement.

Consider proposing at least one of the accompanying terms:

Reexamined Revenue Rates: Solicitation a decrease in financing costs to make the obligation more reasonable.

Expanded Reimbursement Period: Request an augmentation of the reimbursement time frame to decrease the regularly scheduled installment sum.

Obligation Settlement: At times, banks might be available to settle the obligation for a single amount installment that is not exactly all out owed.

Brief Forbearance: Solicitation a transitory suspension or decrease of installments during a time of financial difficulty.

Rebuilding of Debt: Investigate choices for uniting or rebuilding obligation to make it more sensible.

Tailor your proposition to your particular financial conditions, remembering that a thoroughly examined plan improves the probability of lender participation.

4. Experience with Shopper Assurance Laws:

Understanding your freedoms and assurances under shopper security regulations is vital while haggling with lenders. Dive more deeply into applicable regulations, for example, the Fair Debt Collection Practices Act (FDCPA) and other state-explicit guidelines that oversee obligation assortment rehearses.

These regulations furnish buyers with specific privileges, including assurance against provocation, out of line rehearses, and the option to question obligations. Realizing your privileges enables you during discussions and guarantees that lenders comply with lawful rules.

In the event that you accept a bank is disregarding your privileges or participating in unreasonable practices, record the connections and, if fundamental, talk with a legitimate proficient or a shopper security office.

5. Steadiness and Follow-Up:
Haggling with lenders frequently requires steadiness and progressing follow-up. In the event that your underlying proposition isn't acknowledged, cheer up. Loan bosses might require time to audit your proposition or might be available to counteroffers.

Consistently circle back to loan bosses to ask about the situation with your exchange. Be ready to give extra documentation or data whenever mentioned. Tireless and proactive correspondence flags your obligation to settling the obligation and may improve the probability of agreeing.

Also, assuming an understanding is reached, guarantee that the amended terms are plainly archived and recorded as a hard copy. Having a composed understanding safeguards the two players and gives a reference to highlight future corporations.

Haggling with lenders is a complex interaction that requires a mix of financial keen, compelling correspondence, and an essential methodology. By grasping your financial circumstance, conveying transparently, proposing sensible terms, knowing your lawful freedoms, and tirelessly following up, you can expand your possibilities in arriving at a positive goal with banks. Recall that loan bosses are in many cases more ready to work with people who are proactive and helpful in tracking down answers for financial difficulties.

Avoiding Normal Debt Traps

A debt trap implies a snare that happens when a borrower is constrained to take out additional credits to take care of past ones. Basically, a debt trap happens when monetary obligations offset an individual's capacity to reimburse credits.

Payday credits could be one debt trap model, Payday advances are momentary advances with exorbitant financing costs and expenses. Borrowers who can't reimburse on time might take out another credit, prompting a pattern of debt that is difficult to escape.

How Does a Debt Trap Work?

The fundamental credit sum (the sum you get) and the financing cost are two calculations that come into play at whatever point you apply for a line of credit from a moneylender (the sum the bank charges on the chief advance sum). When your chief begins to drop, might you at any point begin pushing ahead with credit reimbursement? In any case, each month that you take care of the credit, you add to both the head and the interest. This is because of the amortizing designs of most credits. This implies that every installment you make towards your credit applies to both the head and the interest, and that your advance is planned to be reimbursed throughout a specific number of fixed portions. Also, on the off chance that you can't make the installment, you are probably going to fall into debt traps.

As it turns out to be truly difficult to take care of your credit in light of the fact that the chief doesn't diminish and the premium continues to gather.

Signs of Debt Trap

1. EMI Compensation Proportion

The EMI compensation proportion is a monetary metric that looks at an individual's month to month credit reimbursement add up to their month to month pay. This proportion decides whether an individual can stand to assume another credit while dealing with their ongoing costs.

For Instance : assuming your EMI is $5000 and your compensation is $15,000 your EMI-pay proportion is 0.5. Experts suggest that proportion ought to be underneath 0.3.

2. Elevated Degrees of Individual Debt

An elevated degree of individual debt, particularly uncollateralized debt like Visas and individual credits, can suggest that people are maintaining an unsustainable lifestyle and might be in danger of falling into a debt trap.

For instance : in the event that an individual has numerous Mastercards and individual credits with high adjusts and battles to make least installments, it can bring about a pattern of getting and exorbitant interest installments.

3. Absence of Monetary Training

An absence of monetary training can make people more powerless against falling into a debt trap, as they might not have the vital information to really deal with their funds.

For instance : On the off chance that an individual gets cash without understanding the premium, time limit, it can prompt a debt trap.

Reasons for Debt Trap

We should look at a couple of reasons that causes debt trap:

1. EMIs Surpass half of Your Pay

Habitual spending could strain your financial plan and wind up making a debt snare for you. In the event that you become an imprudent purchaser and succumb to EMI plans or limits, you become more inclined to falling into a debt trap. In this way, you should be aware of your funds prior to purchasing out of drive.

2. Fixed Costs are More than Your Pay

These days, item promoting is making individuals need things they don't really need. Furthermore, there are a colossal number of monetary organizations prepared to give you credits simply for insignificant documentation. This makes it simple for individuals to spend more than they acquire.

In the event that your decent costs are more than your pay, this may be one more purpose for a debt trap. Taking various credits on the double could cause such a circumstance.

3. Debilitating Credit Breaking point

Mastercard debt is the simplest method for straying into the red snare as a great many people get drawn in by the thrilling offers and engage in ceaseless charge card bills. Then again, Visa organizations charge a considerable amount of interest, which could go from 16 to 32% per annum.

4. Numerous Advances

In the event that you are shuffling numerous individual advances as well as Mastercard charges, you may be short on your everyday costs. In such a circumstance, taking a solitary low-interest individual credit and uniting every one of your credits under one umbrella may be a well conceived plan. It will guarantee opportune reimbursement of your credit and inward feeling of harmony. In any case, taking progressive credits to pay your debts probably won't be such a shrewd decision.

5. No Reimbursement Plan

Visas and credits could look enticing; nonetheless, prior to settling on them, you should think of a reimbursement methodology. Involving an EMI mini-computer for working out your assessed EMI prior to applying for a credit could assist you with arranging your reimbursement system better.

Acquiring may be simple yet reimbursing it can get intense in the event that you don't have a reimbursement plan.

How Does a Credit/Advance Drive the Borrower Into a Debt Trap?

Applying for Visas or credits in a high-risk position could prompt issues or put the borrower in a debt cycle.

For instance, a gourmet expert takes credit for unrefined components for his café, however because of low interest, the singular battles to procure a benefit, so he takes one more credit to recuperate from the misfortune and reimburse the past credit.

Sadly, the singular encounters a similar issue two times and can't reimburse the debt. This is alluded to as a debt trap: a circle of credits that the borrower views as trying to escape.

Avoiding normal debt traps is essential for keeping up with monetary wellbeing and security. Falling into debt traps can prompt a pattern of monetary pressure, making it trying to accomplish long haul monetary objectives. **The following are five critical methodologies to assist you with avoiding normal debt traps:**

1. Budgeting and Financial Planning:

Make a Practical Budget: One of the essential reasons individuals fall into obligation traps is an absence of budgeting. Lay out a definite financial plan that incorporates all kinds of revenue and every single month to month cost. Classify costs into fixed (e.g., lease, utilities) and variable (e.g., food, diversion). Be reasonable and intensive to catch all parts of your financial life.

Emergency Fund: Fabricate and keep an emergency fund to cover surprising costs. Having investment funds put away can forestall dependence on credit cards or advances while confronting abrupt financial difficulties, lessening the gamble of gathering obligation.

Live Inside Your Means: Keep away from the impulse to overspend or enjoy superfluous costs. Separate among needs and needs, and focus on fundamental living costs over optional spending.

2. Understanding Credit and Premium Rates:

Know Your Credit Score: Routinely check your credit score and report to remain informed about your creditworthiness. A decent credit score opens ways to all the more likely loan costs and financial open doors.

Comprehend Revenue Rates: Know about the loan fees related to credit cards, advances, and other financial items. Exorbitant interest obligations can gather rapidly and become a critical weight. Focus on taking care of exorbitant interest obligations to limit long haul financial expenses.

3. Responsible Utilization of Credit Cards:

Keep away from Least Payments: Paying just the base sum due on credit cards can prompt a pattern of obligation. Endeavor to pay the full equilibrium every month to keep away from interest charges.

Limit Credit Card Usage: Use credit cards sensibly and try not to amass balances too far in the red. Consider utilizing money or check cards for routine costs to forestall indiscreet spending.

Understand Terms and Conditions: Comprehend the agreements of your credit cards, including loan costs, charges, and elegance periods. Consciousness of these subtleties can assist you with settling on informed choices and staying away from unforeseen charges.

4. Avoiding Payday Credits and Significant expense Lending:

Investigate Alternatives: As opposed to turning to payday advances or significant expense loaning choices, investigate options like individual advances from legitimate banks, haggling with creditors, or looking for financial help from local area associations.

Comprehend the Risks: Payday credits frequently accompany extravagant financing costs and expenses, driving borrowers into a pattern of obligation. Comprehend the dangers related with such credits and think about elective arrangements.

5. Regular Financial Check-Ups:

Survey and Change Funds Periodically: Consistently audit what is going on and change your systems depending on the situation. Life conditions, for example, work changes or unforeseen costs, may require alterations to your financial arrangement.

Look for Proficient Advice: In the event that you're confronting financial difficulties or taking into account huge financial choices, look for exhortation from financial advocates or experts. They can give direction custom fitted to your circumstance, assisting you with pursuing informed decisions and keep away from potential obligation traps.

By taking on these methodologies, people can proactively deal with their funds and avoid normal obligation traps. Building serious areas of strength for an establishment through budgeting, dependable credit card use, understanding loan fees, keeping away from significant expense loaning, and leading ordinary financial check-ups can add to long haul financial steadiness and security.

Chapter 5: Investing Basics

Prologue to Investing

Investing, extensively, is giving money something to do for a while in a task or undertaking to create positive returns of some kind (i.e., benefits that surpass how much the underlying speculation). It is the demonstration of dispensing assets, generally capital (i.e., money), with the assumption for creating a pay, benefit, or gains.

One can put resources into many sorts of tries (either straightforwardly or by implication) like utilizing money to begin a business, or in resources, for example, buying land in order to produce rental pay or potentially exchanging it later at a more exorbitant cost.

Investing varies from setting aside in that the cash utilized is given something to do, really intending that there is some verifiable gamble that the related project(s) may come up short, bringing about a deficiency of money. Investing likewise varies from hypothesis in that with the last option, the money isn't given something to do essentially, however is wagering on momentary cost vacillations.

KEY Important points

- Investing includes conveying capital (money) toward undertakings or exercises that are supposed to produce a positive return over the long run.

- The sort of profits created relies upon the kind of undertaking or resource; land can deliver the two rents and capital additions; many stocks deliver quarterly profits; bonds will generally pay normal interest.
- In investing, chance and return are two of a kind; okay for the most part implies low anticipated returns, while better yields are typically joined by higher gamble.
- Financial backers can adopt the DIY strategy or utilize the administrations of an expert money director.

Whether purchasing a security qualifies as investing or hypothesis relies upon three variables — how much gamble taken, the holding period, and the cause of profits.

Understanding Investing

Investing is to develop one's money over the long run. The assumption for a positive return as pay or cost appreciation with factual importance is the center reason for investing. The range of resources where one can contribute and procure a return is an exceptionally wide one.

Chance and return remain closely connected in investing; okay for the most part implies low anticipated returns, while better yields are normally joined by higher gamble. At the okay finish of the range are fundamental ventures like Authentications of Store (Compact discs); securities or repaired pay instruments are higher on the gamble scale, while stocks or values are viewed as more hazardous. Products and subordinates are by and large viewed as among the most hazardous speculations. One can likewise put resources into something down to earth, like land or land, or fragile things, like compelling artwork and collectibles.

Chance and return assumptions can change generally inside a similar resource class. For instance, a blue chip that exchanges on the New York Stock Trade will have a totally different gamble return profile from a miniature cap that exchanges on a little trade.

The profits produced by a resource rely upon the kind of resource. For example, many stocks deliver quarterly profits, while bonds by and large compensate for interest each quarter. In numerous purviews, various sorts of pay are charged at various rates.

Notwithstanding standard pay, for example, a profit or interest, value appreciation is a significant part of return. Absolute return from a speculation can in this manner be viewed as the amount of pay and capital appreciation. Standard and Unfortunate gauges that beginning around 1926, profits have contributed almost 33% of absolute value return for the S&P 500 while capital additions have contributed two-thirds.1 Capital increases are accordingly a significant piece of investing.

Financial analysts view investing and saving to be cut out of the same cloth. This is on the grounds that when you set aside cash by saving in a bank, the bank then, at that point, loans that money to people or organizations that need to get that money to effectively utilize it. Thus your reserve funds are many times another person's speculation.

Different Investment Vehicles (Stocks, Bonds, Land, and so on.)

Today, investment is for the most part connected with monetary instruments that permit people or organizations to raise and convey funding to firms. These organizations then, at that point, rake that capital and use it for development or benefit creating exercises.

While the universe of investments is an immense one, here are the most widely recognized sorts of investments:

Stocks

A purchaser of an organization's stock turns into a partial proprietor of that organization. Proprietors of an organization's stock are known as its investors and can partake in its development and accomplishment through appreciation in the stock cost and ordinary profits paid out of the organization's benefits.

Bonds

Bonds are obligation commitments of substances, like states, regions, and organizations. Purchasing a bond suggests that you hold a portion of a substance's obligation and are qualified to get intermittent interest installments and the arrival of the bond's presumptive worth when it develops.

Reserves

Reserves are pooled instruments overseen by investment administrators that empower financial backers to put resources into stocks, bonds, favored shares, products, and so on. Two of the most well-known sorts of assets are common assets and trade exchanged assets or ETFs. Common assets don't exchange on a trade and are esteemed toward the finish of the exchanging day; ETFs exchange on stock trades and, similar to stocks, are esteemed continually all through the exchanging day. Shared assets and ETFs can either latently track files, like the S&P 500 or the Dow Jones Modern Normal, or can be effectively overseen by reserve supervisors.

Investment Trusts

Trusts are one more kind of pooled investment. Real Estate Investment Trusts (REITs) are one of the most famous in this classification. REITs put resources into business or private properties and pay normal circulations to their financial backers from the rental pay received from these properties. REITs exchange on stock trades and accordingly offer their financial backers the benefit of moment liquidity.

Elective Investments

Elective investments is a trick all class that incorporates mutual funds and confidential value. Mutual funds are supposed in light of the fact that they can hedge their investment wagers by going long and short on stocks and different investments. Organizations can raise capital without going public thanks to confidential value. Mutual funds and confidential value were normally simply accessible to prosperous financial backers considered "licensed financial backers" who met specific pay and total assets prerequisites. In any case, as of late, elective investments have been presented in reserve arrangements that are available to retail financial backers.

Choices and Different Subordinates

Subsidiaries are monetary instruments that get their worth from another instrument, like a stock or file. Choices contracts are a famous subsidiary that gives the purchaser the right yet not the commitment to trade a security at a proper cost inside a particular time span. Subsidiaries normally utilize influence, making them a high-risk, high-reward recommendation.

Wares

Items incorporate metals, oil, grain, and creature items, as well as monetary instruments and monetary standards. They can either be exchanged through ware fates — which are arrangements to trade a particular amount of an item at a predefined cost on a specific future date — or ETFs. Products can be utilized for supporting gambling or for theoretical purposes.

Risk Tolerance and Investment Technique

Contributing is an excursion that requires a profound comprehension of one's risk tolerance and a painstakingly created investment technique. The interaction between these two components is essential to building a portfolio that lines up with monetary objectives, time skylines, and individual solace levels. In this thorough investigation, we will dive into the complexities of risk tolerance, the different elements of investment methodology, and the cooperative relationship that exists between them.

1. Understanding Risk Tolerance:

Risk tolerance is a significant figure molding a singular's investment procedure. It addresses the degree of market instability and potential misfortune a financial backer is willing and genuinely ready to persevere. One's risk tolerance is impacted by different elements, including monetary objectives, time skyline, pay solidness, and individual solace with market changes.

Financial backers with high risk tolerance are for the most part more alright with the innate instability of riskier resources, like stocks, and may look for higher expected returns. On the other hand, those with generally safe tolerance might favor more moderate investments, similar to securities or money, to limit openness to showcase changes.

Deciding your risk tolerance implies a legit self-appraisal of your monetary circumstance, mental strength, and investment goals. It's fundamental to adjust your risk tolerance to a reasonable investment procedure to accomplish a harmony between likely returns and the ability to endure market promising and less promising times.

2. Asset Portion as a Risk The board Tool:

Resource portion is a vital part of an investment system that straightforwardly addresses risk tolerance. It includes disseminating your investment portfolio

across various resource classes, like stocks, bonds, and money, to accomplish a harmony among risk and expected reward.

Financial backers with higher risk tolerance might incline towards a more forceful resource distribution, dispensing a bigger piece of their portfolio to values. This technique intends to gain by the development capability of stocks, despite the fact that it accompanies a more elevated level of transient instability.

Then again, financial backers with lower risk tolerance might choose a moderate resource designation, underscoring capital conservation and pay age. This approach normally includes a higher distribution to fixed-pay protections, which are seen as less unstable than stocks.

Consistently rebalancing your portfolio is fundamental to keep up with the ideal resource assignment over the long run. This guarantees that your investments stay lined up with your risk tolerance and monetary objectives, even as economic situations develop.

3. Investment Skyline and Risk Tolerance Alignment:

The investment skyline, or the period of time a financial backer expects to hold their investments, assumes a crucial part in deciding a fitting risk tolerance and investment methodology. Financial backers with a more extended time skyline might have more noteworthy adaptability to weather conditions, transient market variances and are in many cases more qualified to deal with the inborn unpredictability related with riskier resources.

For people with a more drawn out investment skyline, for example, those putting something aside for retirement, a more forceful investment methodology might be reasonable. This might include a higher designation to stocks, which generally have exhibited the potential for long haul capital appreciation notwithstanding intermittent market slumps.

On the other hand, financial backers with a more limited time skyline, like those putting something aside for a close term monetary objective, may focus on capital safeguarding and liquidity. In such cases, a more safe investment approach, with a higher portion to fixed-pay protections, might be desirable to over limit the effect of market unpredictability.

Adjusting your risk tolerance to your investment skyline is fundamental for developing a portfolio that mirrors your monetary goals and time sensitive necessities.

4. Diversification and Risk Mitigation:

Enhancement is a major risk to the executives methodology that implies spreading investments across various resources and areas to lessen the effect of terrible showing in any single investment. Expanded portfolios are intended to moderate risk by staying away from overreliance on a specific resource class or security.

By broadening your investments, you plan to make a stronger portfolio that can endure the high points and low points of different economic situations.

This system is especially important for financial backers with a moderate risk tolerance, looking for a harmony between likely returns and risk relief.

Enhancement stretches out past resource classes and incorporates geographic districts, ventures, and investment styles. A very much differentiated portfolio might incorporate a blend of homegrown and worldwide protections, different businesses, and both development and worth situated investments.

While enhancement doesn't kill risk completely, it assists with overseeing and spreading risk, making it an important device for financial backers trying to adjust their portfolios to their risk tolerance.

5. Regular Survey and Change of Investment Strategy:

Financial backers' risk tolerance isn't static; it can change over the long run because of movements in monetary conditions, life altering situations, or changes in mentality toward risk. Along these lines, it is critical to routinely audit and change your investment system to guarantee it stays lined up with your risk tolerance and monetary objectives.

Occasional reassessment permits you to represent changes in your monetary circumstance, like pay variances, new monetary objectives, or acclimations to your time skyline.

Life altering situations, like marriage, the introduction of a youngster, or approaching retirement, may influence your risk tolerance and require acclimations to your investment procedure.

During market cycles or financial movements, the risk scene can likewise change. Standard surveys give a chance to evaluate the presentation of your investments, think about changes in accordance with your resource distribution, and rebalance your portfolio to keep up with the ideal risk-bring profile back.

Adjusting risk tolerance to a suitable investment methodology is a dynamic and progressing process.

Grasping your risk tolerance, using resource distribution, taking into account your investment skyline, differentiating your portfolio, and routinely exploring and changing your procedure are key parts of a balanced way to deal with overseeing risk in your investment portfolio.

Building a Diversified Investment Portfolio

Building a diversified investment portfolio is a central technique for overseeing risk and streamlining returns. Broadening includes spreading investments across various resource classes, businesses, geographic areas, and sorts of protections to lessen the effect of poor-performing resources on the general portfolio. Here is a complete aide on the most proficient method to fabricate a diversified investment portfolio:

1. Define Your Investment Goals and Risk Tolerance:

Monetary Goals: Obviously articulate your present moment and long haul monetary goals. Whether you're putting something aside for retirement, a home, instruction, or different targets, your goals will shape your investment procedure.

Risk Tolerance: Survey your risk resistance, taking into account your ability to endure market vacillations and your close to home solace with investment risk. Understanding your risk resistance is critical for deciding the blend of resources in your portfolio.

2. Understand Different Resource Classes:

Values (Stocks): Address possession in an organization and proposition the potential for capital appreciation. Values are for the most part thought to be higher risk yet can have serious areas of strength to give over the long haul.

Bonds (Fixed-Pay Securities): Address obligation commitments and deal customary interest installments. Bonds are regularly viewed as lower risk than stocks yet offer lower expected returns.

Real Estate: Putting resources into actual properties or land investment trusts (REITs) can broaden and pay through rental yields.

Endlessly cash Equivalents: Incorporate resources like currency market assets and Depository bills. These give solidness and liquidity however offer lower returns.

3. **Diversify Across Resource Classes:**

Vital Resource Allocation: Decide the ideal blend of resource classes in view of your investment goals, time skyline, and risk resistance. This essential assignment shapes the underpinning of your diversified portfolio.

Rebalance Periodically: Routinely audit and rebalance your portfolio to keep up with the ideal resource allotment. Market developments might cause deviations from your unique arrangement, and rebalancing guarantees that your portfolio stays lined up with your goals.

4. **Diversify Inside Resource Classes:**

Equities: Broaden inside the value piece of your portfolio by putting resources into various areas (innovation, medical services, finance, and so forth) and market capitalizations (huge cap, mid-cap, little cap).

Bonds: Inside the fixed-pay segment, enhance across various security types, for example, government securities, corporate securities, and metropolitan securities. Shift developments to oversee loan cost risk.

Genuine Estate: If consolidating land, consider enhancing across private, business, and modern properties or REITs zeroed in on various areas.

5. Geographic Diversification:

Worldwide Exposure: Consider financial planning internationally to diminish risks related with the exhibition of a solitary economy. Broadening across created and developing business sectors can upgrade portfolio versatility.

Money Exposure: Be aware of cash risk while financial planning universally. Money vacillations can affect the worth of unfamiliar investments.

6. Invest in Various Investment Vehicles:**

Shared Assets and Trade Exchanged Assets (ETFs): These investment vehicles give moment broadening by pooling cash from different financial backers to put resources into a diversified portfolio of stocks, bonds, or different resources.

Individual Stocks and Bonds: In the event that you lean toward an additional active methodology, think about putting resources into individual stocks and bonds. Guarantee that your choice traverses various enterprises and areas.

7. Consider Elective Investments:

Elective Investments: Investigate elective resources like items, mutual funds, or confidential value to add further enhancement. These investments might have low connection with customary resource classes.

Valuable Metals: Including resources like gold or silver can give a fence against expansion and financial vulnerabilities.

8. Monitor and Reassess:

Standard Review: Occasionally survey your portfolio's presentation, monetary circumstances, and any progressions in your monetary circumstance or goals.

Change as Needed: Be ready to make acclimations to your portfolio in light of changes in economic situations or individual conditions. This might include rebalancing, adding new investments, or lessening openness to specific resources.

9. Risk Management:

Risk Assessment: Persistently survey the risk profile of your portfolio. Comprehend the particular risks related with every resource class and pursue informed choices in light of your risk resilience.

Expansion Benefits: Recall that enhancement doesn't dispose of risk altogether, however it oversees and spreads risk, possibly further developing the risk-return profile of your portfolio.

10. Seek Proficient Advice:

Counsel Monetary Advisors: Think about looking for exhortation from monetary experts to fit your investment methodology to your particular goals and risk resistance. Monetary counselors can give customized direction in light of your special conditions.

Building a diversified investment portfolio is a dynamic and progressing process that requires cautious preparation, normal observing, and changes in view of developing conditions. A very much diversified portfolio oversees risk, upgrades security, and positions financial backers to exploit valuable open doors in different economic situations. By grasping your goals, risk resilience, and the different scope of investment choices accessible, you can build a portfolio that lines up with your monetary targets and endures the intricacies of the constantly changing monetary scene.

Chapter 6: Retirement Planning

The Significance of Retirement Planning

Retirement is Inescapable! You can't work for your entire life. Yet, you can guarantee a protected encounter of its vulnerability by adding your retirement planning to your need list.

Retirement might feel like a world away to a few of us, so we don't frequently consider it. In any case, neglecting to plan or save for the future might bring about monetary worries. Also, neglecting to take advantage of your time right now may bring about a few botched open doors, like the advantages of self multiplying dividends.

Furthermore, in this article, we will zero in on how retirement planning empowers you to take advantage of your post-retirement life.

What is retirement planning?

Retirement planning alludes to making key courses of action and creating plans for the future tomorrow. It permits you to be monetarily steady and autonomous even after retirement. With retirement planning, you can in any case meet and accomplish your generally unimaginable objectives. Retirement plans contrast from each other in light of the fact that each individual has their novel objectives and dreams they need to achieve. Furthermore, that is the reason you ought to plan a retirement plan that meets impeccably with your requirements and future desires.

Justifications for why retirement planning is important

You resign from your work, not life. Along these lines, while you may not be working any longer, you actually could have a few objectives you might want to achieve post-retirement. All the while, you would likewise need to keep up with and balance your life like before without worrying about your everyday uses.

By planning, you can make a daily existence brimming with solace where you are not reliant upon anybody. So let us take a gander at the seven justifications for why you really want to have retirement planning in your life and how it can assist you with planning for later:

1. To get ready for a more drawn out life

The typical future is higher today. In this way, you want to save a lot for the costs if you have any desire to help yourself post-retirement. Through advance retirement planning, you can make courses of action to have long post-retirement funds and keep yourself from turning out to be financially reliant upon your kids. Trust me when I say this that Banks won't be supporting you.

2. To keep up with your way of life

I'm certain you would need to keep living and supporting your current way of life even after you have resigned and quit working. As of now, you don't need to stress over your way of life in light of the fact that your compensation covers your day to day and recreation costs like going out for supper at the end of the week, repeating lengthy drives, venturing to every part of the nation/world, and so on. However, after you resign, just retirement planning assists you with keeping a customary pay to help your way of life and keep up with the ongoing way of life.

3. To be prepared for a crisis

Clinical costs or monetary crises won't sit tight for you to settle down or check out at your monetary wellbeing prior to striking. You would have no desire to be subject to anybody in these circumstances. Today, you have the freedom to get cash utilizing an Individual Credit or even get from your Companions/Family/Boss, yet after retirement, none of these choices may be open. Thus, sound retirement planning enables you to deal with your monetary record and remain free financially in any event, during difficult stretches in your life.

4. To abandon an inheritance

We as a whole invested some parcel of energy, all day, every day, to give an agreeable way of life to our loved ones. Furthermore, you would need to ensure that it will keep going for the next few years ahead, regardless of whether you are not there with everybody. Along these lines, when you have your retirement planning to fabricate your post-retirement investment funds, you can likewise abandon abundance for your relatives. It will end up being your inheritance and help the new ages during startling emergencies.

5. To battle expansion

With the consistent ascent in assistance and merchandise costs, our way of life is getting impacted. Supper in an eatery used to cost 800-1000 for 2 individuals around a long time back, today it costs very nearly 1500-1800 in a city like Bangalore, what you could purchase today at a particular cost would cost significantly more tomorrow. Furthermore, it would essentially affect your life post-retirement; consequently, only putting something aside for your retirement probably won't help; all things considered, you'll need to design and grasp the specific necessities for your retirement. You can start effective financial planning now to develop your cash and route expansion.

6. To satisfy your future objectives

As referenced before, your retirement doesn't spell almost certain doom for your life. You have just quit working. We comprehend that your ongoing life objectives probably won't give you a significant chance to carry on with your life; subsequently, you don't have to abandon everything you could ever hope for or objectives that you harbor inside you. Post-retirement, you have a lot of extra energy to satisfy your goals. It may very well be sending your kid to concentrate abroad, get voyaging, or seek after another leisure activity. Furthermore, you can achieve every one of them through your monetary planning and financial reserve funds.

7. To forestall making critical get up to speed commitments

You can't turn your head and say that I won't ever resign. A retired person who makes installments north of 30 years might have the option to develop bigger retirement investment funds than a retired person who begins consistently contributing just a brief time before retirement. You can fabricate your retirement reserves rapidly by placing a huge load of cash into make up for lost time commitments. Be that as it may, for the vast majority, it's more straightforward to save a more modest aggregate north of quite a long while instead of expecting to rapidly get the ball really rolling. Accumulate interest additionally becomes an integral factor on the grounds that the more drawn out the window for conceivable improvement is, the prior you can contribute.

Things to remember while planning for retirement:

Allow us momentarily to go through certain elements that we ought to bear in mind while we are planning our retirement planning:

- **Screen your speculations consistently:**

Returns are not true to form all of the time. In this way, it will assist you with planning effectively for your retirement and settle on speedy and sane choices.

- **Draw your speculations nearer to retirement:**

You can move your ventures to bring down risk decisions when you are crawling nearer to retirement. It helps in diminishing your value openness.

- **Include your family and get ready desk work ahead of time:**

It is smarter to keep your family mindful of the fundamental desk work and money related subtleties for your retirement planning. It is valuable when you face an unexpected direness or a sad circumstance.

- **Pick the confided in accomplice:**

Retirement planning isn't something straightforward and accommodating. Your future and cash rely upon it; in this way, you ought to continuously work with confided in accomplices as it were. It guarantees that your cash matters are in safe hands.

- **Start early:**

Time is essential to your retirement planning. Consequently, the prior you start, the additional time you need to develop your cash to satisfy more dreams.

The speculation precedes spending: Fix your resources two or three days after you get your month to month compensation. It permits you to protect your use rate and venture reserves without a hitch.

- **Take care of your credits first:**

Before your retirement planning, you can guide your reserve funds to take care of your advances first (particularly when you have a higher loan fee). It keeps your retirement from falling into liabilities.

- **Have programmed moves:**

One can make your speculations more open by setting up programmed bank moves. It assists you with staying away from any misses in a month or postponements in paying.

In this way, presently you comprehend the advantages of a post-retirement plan. What's more, the various ways it is crucial for getting a superior future for yourself as well as your loved ones. In the present time, retirement planning is very critical for everybody. It gives you the power and position to oversee and control your life even after you have quit working. You can profit from different advantages like expense alleviation and wellbeing claims that assist with making your life tranquil.

You can likewise get some margin to tick off the left-out things on your list of must-dos and seek after free living without expecting to auction your properties and resources. In this way, the earlier you put resources into your retirement plan, the additional time you get to set aside cash and carry on with an existence with solace and security.

Types of Retirement Accounts (401(k), IRA, and so forth.)

There are a few kinds of retirement accounts, each offering extraordinary duty benefits, commitment cutoff points, and withdrawal rules. These accounts are intended to assist people with putting something aside for retirement and give a type of revenue during their retirement years. Here are a portion of the normal sorts of retirement accounts:

1. 401(k) Plans:

A 401(k) is a business supported retirement reserve funds plan. Workers contribute a part of their pre-charge compensation to the arrangement, and bosses might match a piece of those commitments. Commitments develop charge conceded until withdrawal. There are customary 401(k) plans where commitments are made pre-duty, and Roth 401(k) plans where commitments are made after-charge, yet qualified withdrawals are tax-exempt.

2. Individual Retirement Accounts (IRAs):

IRAs are private retirement investment accounts that people can open with a monetary foundation. There are two principal sorts of IRAs:

Customary IRA: Commitments to a conventional IRA might be charge deductible, and income develop charge conceded until withdrawal. Nonetheless, withdrawals in retirement are burdened as common pay.

Roth IRA: Commitments to a Roth IRA are made with after-charge dollars, and qualified withdrawals, including income, are tax-exempt. Roth IRAs don't need least conveyances (RMDs), making them appealing for the people who need greater adaptability in retirement.

3. Rollover IRAs:

A Rollover IRA is a sort of conventional IRA that permits people to merge assets from boss supported retirement plans, for example, 401(k) or 403(b), while changing position or resigning. Turning over assets into an IRA can give more command over venture decisions.

4. SEP IRA (Worked on Representative Benefits IRA):

A SEP IRA is intended for entrepreneurs and independently employed people. It permits commitments to be made by the business in the interest of qualified workers, and commitments are charge deductible. SEP IRAs offer adaptability in commitment sums and are not difficult to set up.

5. Simple IRA (Investment funds Motivator Match Plan for Employees):

Like a SEP IRA, a Basic IRA is intended for private companies. The two bosses and representatives can make commitments. Commitments are charge deductible, and the arrangement is moderately simple for private ventures to regulate.

6. 403(b) Plans:

A 403(b) plan is like a 401(k) yet is accessible to workers of specific duty excluded associations, government funded schools, and philanthropic associations. Workers can make pre-charge commitments, and a few managers might offer matching commitments.

7. 457(b) Plans:

A 457(b) plan is a retirement plan accessible to specific government and non-legislative workers. Commitments to a 457(b) plan are made on a pre-charge premise, and the arrangement might take into consideration extra get up to speed commitments for those near retirement.

8. Thrift Investment funds Plan (TSP):

The Frugality Investment funds Plan is a retirement investment funds plan for government workers, including individuals from the military. Like a 401(k), representatives can make commitments on a pre-expense or Roth premise, and the public authority might give matching commitments to specific workers.

9. Profit-Sharing Plans:

Benefit sharing plans are business supported retirement designs that permit bosses to add to their representatives' retirement reserve funds in light of the organization's benefits. Commitments are optional, giving businesses adaptability in adding to the arrangement.

10. Defined Benefit Plans:

Not at all like characterized commitment plans, for example, 401(k)s, characterized benefit plans guarantee a particular benefit sum at retirement. Bosses add to the arrangement and are answerable for guaranteeing that there are adequate assets to meet the guaranteed benefits.

Each sort of retirement account has its own standards, benefits, and contemplations. It's fundamental for people to pick retirement accounts that line up with their monetary objectives, business circumstance, and chance resilience. Talking with a monetary consultant can give customized direction in light of individual conditions.

Maximizing Employer Benefits

To maximize employer benefits, employees should thoroughly understand available offerings, including health insurance, retirement plans, and wellness programs. Contribute to retirement plans to take advantage of employer matching, utilize wellness benefits, and explore flexible spending accounts. Actively engage with HR resources for optimal utilization and financial well-being.

1. Understanding and Utilizing Retirement Benefits:

Employer-sponsored retirement benefits, such as 401(k) plans, represent a valuable opportunity for employees to build long-term financial security. To maximize these benefits, it's crucial to understand the employer's contribution matching policy and strive to contribute enough to take full advantage of the match. For example, if the employer matches contributions up to a certain percentage of salary, employees should aim to contribute at least that amount to maximize the employer's financial contribution to their retirement savings.

2. Exploring Health and Wellness Benefits:

Employers often provide a range of health and wellness benefits, including health insurance, dental plans, and wellness programs. Maximizing these benefits involves carefully reviewing plan options, understanding coverage details, and selecting plans that align with individual health needs. Additionally, taking advantage of wellness programs, such as gym memberships or preventive health screenings, can contribute to overall well-being and potentially reduce out-of-pocket healthcare costs.

3. Leveraging Flexible Spending Accounts (FSAs) and Health Savings Accounts (HSAs):

Many employers offer FSAs and HSAs to help employees manage healthcare expenses. Maximizing these accounts involves contributing the maximum allowable amount, taking advantage of tax advantages, and planning expenses to use funds efficiently. FSAs are typically used for qualified medical expenses, while HSAs offer a triple tax advantage—contributions are tax-deductible, earnings grow tax-free, and withdrawals for qualified medical expenses are tax-free.

4. Participating in Employee Stock Purchase Plans (ESPPs):

Employee Stock Purchase Plans allow employees to purchase company stock at a discounted price. Maximizing this benefit involves participating in the ESPP and taking advantage of the discounted purchase price. Employees should carefully review plan details, contribution limits, and holding periods to make informed decisions about when to buy and sell company stock. Diversifying investments beyond company stock is also advisable to manage risk.

5. Capitalizing on Professional Development Opportunities:

Employers often invest in professional development and education for their employees. Maximizing these opportunities involves actively seeking out training programs, workshops, and courses that align with career goals. Taking advantage of tuition reimbursement programs, if available, can further enhance skills and qualifications without incurring significant personal expenses.Proactively examining proficient improvement with managers and partaking in mentorship projects can show a guarantee to vocation development and may prompt extra progression open doors inside the association.

Strategies for Catching Up on Retirement Savings

We maintain that you should hear us say this: Beginning putting something aside for retirement is rarely past the point of no return. Regardless of how old you are or how much (or how little) you have saved up to this point, there's continuously something you can do. You can't change the past, yet you can in any case change your future. The fat woman hasn't sung at this point!

As per The Province of Individual budget study, the greater part of Americans are not at present money management for the future, and, surprisingly, more (60%) feel behind on their retirement investment funds objectives.

Now is the ideal time to awaken, individuals! However, don't allow that alert to alarm you. We will stroll through a couple of ways you can get up to speed with your retirement reserve funds together.

On the off chance that you're reluctant to take a look at your 401(k) equilibrium or feel tragically behind with regards to putting something aside for retirement, refocusing is not past the point of no return!

Suppose you're 40 years of age with a $55,000 pay and nothing put something aside for retirement. We suggest you save 15% of your gross pay for retirement, and that implies you ought to put $688 every month into your 401(k) and IRA. Assuming you did that for a considerable length of time, you could wind up breaking the $1 million imprint at age 65. Truth be told — you would be a tycoon!

Be that as it may, imagine a scenario in which you're 45. For sure assuming that you're as of now in your 50s? Here's where you can exploit your age.

Individuals matured 45-54 are hitting their pinnacle procuring years, with the run of the mill family pay floating around $97,000 a year.1 Assuming you contribute 15% of that, you'll take care of $14,550 per year for retirement!

Assuming you keep fixed on your retirement dream and keep effective financial planning that sum consistently for a long time, you could have more than $1 million put aside for retirement! That is the force of time and accumulating funds at work. You can run a few numbers for yourself with our venture mini-computer, which will do all the math for you.

1. Increment Commitments to Retirement Accounts:

One compelling technique for making up for lost time with retirement reserve funds is to expand commitments to retirement accounts. Exploit commitment limits for boss supported plans like 401(k)s and individual retirement accounts (IRAs). For those matured 50 and more established, there are make up for lost time commitments permitted, empowering bigger yearly commitments.

Expanding commitments step by step over the long run, particularly while getting pay raises, can assist with limiting the effect on current funds. It's crucial for audit and change commitments routinely to guarantee they line up with retirement objectives.

2. Expand Business Matching Contributions:

On the off chance that a business offers a matching commitment to retirement accounts, boosting this benefit is pivotal. Contribute to the point of fitting the bill for the full manager match, as this addresses a prompt and significant lift to retirement reserve funds. Neglecting to exploit manager matches is basically overlooking free cash.

Understanding the business' matching approach and endeavoring to contribute essentially the matched sum can fundamentally speed up the development of retirement reserves.

3. Consider Deferring Retirement:

For people who are behind on retirement investment funds, expanding the functioning years can be a useful procedure. Postponing retirement considers extra long stretches of pay, commitments to retirement records, and expected development in speculations. Besides, postponing the beginning of Federal retirement aide advantages can bring about higher regularly scheduled installments when ultimately guaranteed.

This technique requires cautious thought of individual wellbeing, position fulfillment, and generally speaking monetary circumstance. It's fundamental to assess whether proceeding to work is possible and lines up with one's drawn out objectives.

4. Cut Pointless Costs and Increment Savings:

Surveying and advancing current ways of managing money is a viable method for opening up assets for retirement investment funds. Distinguish insignificant costs that can be diminished or disposed of, and divert those assets toward retirement accounts. Fostering a financial plan can give a reasonable picture of where cash is being spent and recognize regions for possible reserve funds.

As well as cutting superfluous costs, consider allocating bonuses or rewards straightforwardly to retirement reserve funds. This incorporates charge discounts, work rewards, or any surprising monetary benefits.

5. Investigate Extra Revenue Streams:

Producing extra pay through side gigs, temporary work, or independent open doors can contribute altogether to getting up to speed with retirement investment funds. The gig economy offers different choices for acquiring additional pay, whether through counseling, independent composition, coaching, or different abilities.

Enhancing normal pay with extra streams can make a monetary pad devoted to retirement reserve funds. It's vital to apportion the extra pay admirably and focus on commitments to retirement accounts.

6. Look for Proficient Monetary Advice:

Talking with a monetary consultant is a judicious step for those hoping to get up to speed with retirement reserve funds. A monetary expert can survey what is happening, put forth practical retirement objectives, and foster a custom-made system to accomplish them.

A monetary consultant can give direction on venture decisions, charge suggestions, and by and large retirement arranging. Having a thoroughly examined plan and master exhortation can impart certainty and set people on the correct way toward a safer retirement.

Making up for lost time with retirement reserve funds requires a blend of proactive techniques, including expanding commitments, boosting boss advantages, taking into account deferred retirement, cutting pointless costs, investigating extra revenue sources, and looking for proficient monetary guidance. Executing these techniques on the whole can altogether upgrade retirement prospects in any event, for those beginning later in their reserve funds venture.

Chapter 7: Creating Additional Income Streams

Hustles and Freelancing

Creating additional income streams is a strategic approach to enhance financial stability and achieve long-term financial goals. Diversifying sources of income not only provides a safety net in times of economic uncertainty but also accelerates wealth-building.

Hustles and freelancing have become popular ways for individuals to diversify their income, pursue passion projects, and gain financial independence. Whether you're looking to make extra money on the side or transition to a full-time freelance career, here are key aspects to consider:

1. Side Hustles and Freelancing: Engaging inside hustles or freelance work allows individuals to monetize skills outside of their primary profession. This could include consulting, writing, graphic design, or other talents.

2. Investing in Real Estate: Real estate investments, whether through rental properties or real estate crowdfunding platforms, can generate passive income and potential appreciation over time.

3. Dividend Stocks and Investments: Investing in dividend-paying stocks or funds provides a steady income stream through periodic dividend distributions, contributing to both income and portfolio growth.

4. Online Businesses: Starting an online business, such as e-commerce, blogging, or affiliate marketing, can generate income through advertising, product sales, or affiliate partnerships.

5. Rental Income from Assets: Renting out assets like equipment, vehicles, or even unused space can generate additional income without a significant time commitment.

6. Consulting or Coaching: Sharing expertise through consulting or coaching services can be a lucrative way to leverage professional skills for additional income.

7. Creating and Selling Products: Developing and selling products, whether physical or digital, on platforms like Etsy or Amazon, offers an avenue for creative individuals to generate income.

8. Part-Time or Gig Work: Taking on part-time or gig work in areas like ride-sharing, delivery services, or pet sitting can provide immediate income without a long-term commitment.

9. Teaching and Tutoring: Offering tutoring services or teaching online courses on platforms like Udemy or Skillshare can turn expertise into a source of income.

10. Monetizing Hobbies: Turning hobbies into income-generating activities, such as photography, crafting, or music, provides a fulfilling way to earn extra money.

By diversifying income streams, individuals not only create financial resilience but also open doors to new opportunities for growth and wealth accumulation. The key is to align additional income pursuits with personal interests and skills to maximize both financial and personal satisfaction.

Side Passive Income Opportunities

There are a wide range of justifications for why you might be searching for better approaches to bring in cash on the web, and fortunately there are more open doors than any other time in recent memory to do this in the present economy. With expansion high and financing costs climbing, your cash isn't extending to the extent that it once did. However, there are ways of utilizing the web to acquire new revenue sources and assist with supporting your funds.

What's more, that is valid whether you're searching for ways of enhancing your income or need to track down a totally new vocation way. Generally speaking, you might in fact utilize your current abilities to make an automated source of income.

In any case, given the large number of choices you need to bring in cash on the web, it could be challenging to sort out which valuable open doors are genuine, will not need a lot of cash forthright — and are ideal for you. To assist you with getting everything rolling, we've gathered together the absolute most effective ways to begin making recurring, automated revenue at the present time.

Automated revenue is basically cash you're making from a source or business other than your immediate manager. This sort of pay is frequently procured through an undertaking or activity performed on your standard work that doesn't need a ton of work to do (which is the reason a significant number of these pay sources are viewed as on the web).

All things considered, notwithstanding its name, even automated revenue can take some work, both forthright and continuous.

"Loosened up rehearses recall exchange or strategic policies for which you don't undeniably share. You truly partake in a development if you're locked in with the action of the activity for a common, constant, and critical reason," the IRS figures out on its site.

Coming up next are 10 unique ways you can use a repetitive kind of revenue to bring in some extra cash.

1. Take online outlines

Giving your perspective and participating in factual studying can be a straightforward technique for getting cash on the web. A piece of the more popular survey regions consolidate Study Junkie, Swagbucks, OneOpinion, Evaluation Station and Ipsos iSay.

Sort out how you can make two or three extra bucks from home by taking web based audits now!

Keep in mind: This kind of repeating, robotized income won't get massive benefits, but it can put some extra cash in your pocket. Swagbucks says its people get about $1 to $5 every day generally speaking. Basically guarantee you really do some assessment before you start or spotlight on partaking in any electronic outlines.

2. Seek after a gig-working stage

For online gig work, there are a couple of stages planned.For example, Amazon Mechanical Turk is a site you can use to take on little tasks for associations across the globe. They could consolidate coordinating substance, taking an outline or deciphering sound.

Clickworker is a relative stage, then again if you have a specific mastery — like copywriting, modifying or visual correspondence — you can use re-appropriating stages like Fiverr, Freelancer.com and Upwork to interact with anticipated clients.

Advancement

3. Start a blog

Sites aren't so much for not a really obvious explanation specifically these days. They can be a wonderful mother lode when gotten along admirably. The best approach to making a productive blog is to pick your claim to fame, create your group and subsequently adjust. Building a following can take some time nonetheless, so show restrictions.

You can do this through part displaying, which obtains you a commission when someone clicks an adjusted association or buys a thing that is progressed on your blog. You could moreover have a go at selling and showing advancements on your site using a gadget like Google Adsense.

4. Start an online store

In case you're the imaginative kind, you ought to genuinely consider selling your items online through a site like Etsy. Traders on Etsy offer everything from embellishments and dress to craftsmanship, requesting yard signs, designs and that is only the start.

You could attempt to choose to start a re-appropriating store, which is fundamentally a client confronting exterior. Exactly when a client makes a solicitation, you demand that thing from an outcast (a producer, trader, or distributor) and ship it clearly to the client.

5. Start a YouTube channel

YouTube producers can make mountains of money, and starting doesn't ensure a great deal of dominance. You can make how-to or explainer accounts on basically any subject, or go more private and set yourself in the accounts. Consider different arrangements that are productive on the stage, like talking very much educated specialists, giving tips and hoodwinks, or even appearing yourself playing changed video, compact or prepackaged games.

Like composition for a blog, the huge thing is to find a claim to fame and build a following. You can then organize Google Advancements, become a YouTube Associate, and in any event, get cash off enlistments, live visits and enrollments.

6. Acquire cash from photography

In the event that you're known as the visual expert in the family, you can obtain some additional cash by selling your photographs on the web. There are locales like Creative work America in which you can move your photos and have them featured on stock that is sold on the site.

7. Transform into a transcriptionist

If you're a fast typer, you ought to truly consider doing some online records for cash. You'll essentially need to focus on sound records and subsequently definitively type out what you hear. You get repaid per piece, so the speedier you can type, the better concerning acquiring cash. Rev.com, GoTranscript and TranscribeMe are several districts where you can find online record work.

8. Turn into a remote helper

More work than any other time is being done web based following the new ascent in remote work. It seems OK, then, at that point, that remote assistance is more normal, as well. By turning into a menial helper through sites Quite like (simply look for "Far off Remote helper") you can work for a business deprived from the solace of your work space.

The work required changes — you could find gigs going from keeping in touch with online entertainment the board to conventional accounting — so search for something that accommodates your abilities and foundation.

9. Test sites and applications

Extravagant yourself, the well informed type? Provided that this is true, you can get compensated to try out new sites and versatile applications and chase down any errors. At UserTesting.com, for instance, you get the chance to test new destinations and items from famous brands today.

You basically must have a reliable Remote affiliation, a beneficiary, a PC or cell and you can get to work. BetaTesting.com, UserZoom and Userlytics are other equivalent stages.

10. Trade area names

Those with also web-shrewd abilities should seriously think about recurring, automated revenue by means of buying and afterward selling area names. Locals like GoDaddy.com might actually assist with finishing the deal by means of an internet based closeout. Or on the other hand basically purchase names you think might be fascinating from here on out (think diversion, sports and political occasions) then, at that point, put your contact data on those URLs and propose to offer them to anybody hoping to purchase.

There's a part time job for everybody; you simply have to sort out your ideal fit. Begin with a thought above, then think about stretching out regardless of whether your most memorable give work a shot. Like any kind of pay, creating a strong wellspring of recurring, automated revenue can take some forthright time and exertion. Meanwhile, you can begin little and start bringing in cash by taking reviews now. Reviews are one fast and simple method for making some additional money in your margin time.

Investing in income producing assets

A magnificent point along the monetary strengthening venture is understanding that, generally, cash coming in is more noteworthy than cash going out. This is a marvelous achievement that everybody ought to be exceptionally pleased with. The place of supported positive income is generally owing to difficult work, inspiration, and courage to lay out sound cash propensities. Presently you will end up confronting another significant monetary choice - how would I manage this additional cash? The time has come to begin getting a few resources! The following are two significant standards to assist with directing your choice

Not All Resources are made equivalent

Pay Delivering Resources > Pay Consuming Resources

Quite possibly your main decision whenever you've dominated individual income is focusing on pay delivering resources over pay consuming resources. Pay delivering resources create income for you, while pay consuming resources require income from you.

How about we require this subsequent rule: Pay Creating Resources > Pay Consuming Resources. The justification behind this is straightforward - pay delivering resources can possibly increase abundance after some time, while pay consuming resources decline abundance over the long run. Pay consuming resources ought not be totally dismissed - all things considered, the difficult work and exertion you put in to acquire pay and live financially dependable additionally incorporates purchasing resources that give delight and joy. In view of that, we should investigate the distinction between these two resource types and a few hints to assist with striking a solid monetary and individual equilibrium.

What are pay delivering resources?

Pay creating resources are ventures that produce income for you. Instances of pay creating resources incorporate investment properties, profit paying stocks, securities, and shared reserves. At the point when you put resources into a pay creating resource, you can hope to get an ordinary stream of pay from that speculation.

One of the greatest benefits of pay creating resources is that they can give a wellspring of recurring, automated revenue. That implies you can bring in cash without having to work for it effectively. In the event that you're hoping to create financial stability over the long haul, having a wellspring of automated revenue can be a tremendous assistance.

One more benefit of pay delivering resources is that they can give a fence against expansion. At the point when costs ascend over the long haul, the worth of your money possessions will diminish. Notwithstanding, in the event that you own pay creating resources, the pay they produce might ascend alongside expansion.

The following are not many instances of pay creating resources

1. Currency market account

A currency market account (MMA) is somewhat of a half and half. It falls somewhere close to conventional financial records and an exorbitant premium bank account. Like financial records, you can get to your record with a check card. The thing that matters is that you'll acquire revenue on the assets in the record. MMAs are accessible through banks and credit associations and are not difficult to open. The premium acquired on the record changes in view of market variances. Because of how fluid MMA is, it's an amazing choice for reserves you've taken care of for a crisis.

The drawback is that MMAs don't procure the financing costs you'll track down in other, less secure speculations. The potential gain is that the FDIC guarantees the assets in a MMA.

Risk level: Low

2. Authentication of store

Another protected pay producing resource is a declaration of store (Disc). A Disc is a sort of time store, meaning you should leave your cash in the record for a pre-set period to procure the guaranteed financing cost. A Disc is similar to a bank account, with two massive contrasts. In the first place, you can't pull out the assets before the Compact disc develops without punishment. The second is that Cds regularly have a higher financing cost than you can procure with a customary bank account.

Suppose you buy a two-year Compact disc with a loan cost of 1.5%. To procure that 1.5% on the assets, you'll have to leave them in the record for quite a long time. In the event that you pull out the cash early, a punishment will be expected.

Risk level: Low

3. Stocks

Suppose you buy 100 offers in the Top Block Organization for $10 each. On the off chance that Zenith gets along nicely and benefits are up, the worth of your portions goes up. In the event that Top runs into a difficult situation and benefits are down, the worth of your portions goes down. You could lose the whole $1,000 contributed in the event that things get genuinely horrendous.

Individuals put resources into explicit organizations by buying stock since they've explored the business and accept it will find success. At the point when they're correct, the worth of their stock increments.

A few organizations likewise deliver profits, and that implies they share a piece of their benefits with investors. Holding portions of a fruitful business' stock method partaking in the pay related to profits. You can utilize the money to pay everyday costs, reinvest it, or whatever else you'd like.

Purchasing individual stocks ought not be mistaken for putting resources into shared reserves. At the point when you put resources into a common asset, your cash goes toward purchasing stocks from a few organizations. Like that, assuming one of the organizations does a plunge, you generally have different organizations to support the worth of your record. While common assets are not without chances, they are safer than holding individual stocks.

Risk level: By and large, the securities exchange has gotten along admirably, yet there are no assurances of future execution. You risk losing your venture.

4. Real estate

There are multiple ways putting resources into real estate can turn out revenue.

Purchasing property

Buying real estate and involving it as investment property is one method for producing pay, however it's not without expected issues. For instance, you might get tenants who oftentimes miss installments or purchase a home that persistently needs fixes. In any case, possessing real estate can be productive for those able to put time and cash into a pay creating resource.

Risk level: Medium: Things could go one way or the other. The redeeming quality is that you have the property to exchange if necessary.

REIT

In the event that you'd prefer not to be so involved, you can put resources into a Real Estate Speculation Trust (REIT). Like a shared asset, a REIT puts resources into various real estate types, similar to places of business, stockpiling units, parking structures, and high rises. Furthermore, as common assets, the dangers related with a REIT are fanned out. Regardless of whether a couple of the ventures perform well, there's an opportunity the others will.

Risk level: Hazardous: How productive real estate is relies upon factors like loan costs and the economy in general. You can rely on variances and may lose your venture.

Crowdfunding

Another pay producing resource choice is real estate crowdfunding. Basically, crowdfunding includes adding your venture to a pool of cash from different financial backers. You realize ahead of time which kind of property you're putting resources into. For instance, it could be private lodging, business property, or retail space. When you contribute, you own a portion of the holding.

Risk level: Hazardous: Borrowers are not expected to buy and by ensuring the advance, meaning you could lose your venture on the off chance that things kick the bucket.

5. Shared lending

Individuals denied bank advances frequently go to distributed (P2P) moneylenders to get. As a P2P bank, you get to conclude which credits you're willing to make and don't need to finance the whole credit all alone. For instance, you might stumble into somebody who needs to get $10,000. You could credit the entire sum or a piece of it. Assuming that different moneylenders get the rest, the credit application is supported.

Prior to concluding which advance you might want to assist with, you will have admittance to data about the borrower, including their financial assessment. The less secure the credit, the more premium the borrower is charged and the more premium you can acquire. In the event that you'd like to stay with lower-risk credits, you'll in any case procure revenue at a lower rate.

Risk level: Moderate: You keep up with some control with P2P credits by picking which advances to partake in.

In any case, a few borrowers will break their agreements by not paying, and in light of the fact that no guarantee is involved, it's basically impossible to recover your misfortune.

Other pay creating resources remember effective money management for farmland, annuities, and securities. Prior to effective financial planning, however, get your work done.

Investigate the general mishmash of every expected venture. It depends on you to decide your gamble resistance and which speculations best fit your style.

What are pay consuming resources?

Pay consuming resources are
speculations that require income from you. Instances of pay consuming resources incorporate your home, vehicle, and other individual belongings. At the point when you put resources into a pay consuming resource, you can hope to burn through cash on upkeep, fixes, and different costs related to that venture.

One of the greatest detriments of pay consuming resources is that they can be a channel on your funds. In the event that you own a vehicle, for instance, you'll need to pay for things like fuel, upkeep, fixes, and protection. These costs can accumulate over the long haul and remove a critical piece from your financial plan.

One more burden of pay consuming resources is that they create no pay for you. All things considered, they expect you to burn through cash on them. This actually intends that assuming you're attempting to create financial wellbeing over the long haul, pay consuming resources won't assist you with accomplishing that objective.

Very much like pay creating resources can be a fence against expansion, pay consuming resources can worsen the adverse consequences of expansion.

So what is the contention for purchasing pay consuming resources?
All things considered, Let's be real, I'm not a machine - I'm an individual... an individual who appreciates going on outings, showing up for shows, purchasing presents for loved ones, and having a really agreeable lounge chair to peruse the most recent Normal Pennies article. Like such countless things in money and effective financial planning, balance is critical and the underneath contemplations can assist you with finding the right equilibrium of pay consuming resources for your life.

Need:
Some pay consuming resources, like a home or a vehicle, are essential for everyday residing. In these cases, it very well might be important to purchase pay consuming resources, regardless of whether they create pay for you.

Individual happiness:
Some pay consuming resources, for example, a summer home or a boat, and show passes might be bought fundamentally for individual pleasure. While these resources may not produce pay, they can give critical delight and unwinding, which is a significant piece of life! Be careful, the twist of web-based entertainment on the meaning of individual delight. Consistent correlation with misleading and unrealistic assumptions for reality can trap us into spending more on things to intrigue others than for individual satisfaction.

Tax cuts:

Some pay consuming resources, like a main living place or a beneficent gift, may give tax reductions that can balance the expense of proprietorship. For instance, the interest you pay on your home loan might be charge deductible, which can lessen your general expense risk.

Prior to putting resources into pay producing resources, it's significant to lead exhaustive exploration, survey risk resilience, and think about the general venture technique. Enhancing across various resource classes can assist with overseeing risk and improve the potential for consistent pay over the long haul. Furthermore, talking with a monetary counsel can give customized direction in light of individual monetary objectives and conditions.

Entrepreneurial Ventures

Entrepreneurial ventures are frequently begun by people energetic about tackling issues and setting out new open doors. Be that as it may, scaling a venture can be testing — it tends to be hard to grow a business quickly while keeping up with its guiding principle and culture. As a business expert who has effectively scaled many ventures, notwithstanding, I have found that few key variables can assist organizations with accomplishing this. The following are seven moves toward considering executing on the off chance that you haven't as of now.

1. Foster a reasonable development technique.

To scale effectively, you want to have an unmistakable development technique that incorporates explicit objectives, timetables and measurements. Your technique ought to likewise recognise possible difficulties and amazing open doors that might emerge during the development cycle.

2. Construct areas of strength

Scaling a business requires a group of devoted and capable people who share similar vision and values as your organization. Employ individuals who are energetic about your central goal and have what it takes to assist you with accomplishing your objectives.

While figuring out who might be areas of strength for a player during the employing system, consider the singular's experience working in a group climate. Is it safe to say that they were ready to add to the group's prosperity, convey successfully, and cooperate with other people? Also, asking social meeting inquiries focusing on cooperation can empower significant bits of knowledge to work really with others.

3. Encourage a culture of development.

Making a climate that upholds trial and error and chance taking can assist with rousing colleagues to consider new ideas and foster effective fixes. By focusing on a culture of development, groups can open their maximum capacity and assist with driving significant advancement forward. Urge your group to be imaginative and creative in their way to deal with critical thinking by effectively searching out and empowering cooperation and meetings to generate new ideas, giving open doors to proficient turn of events, and encouraging a climate where disappointment is seen as a growth opportunity as opposed to a misfortune.

4. Influence innovation.

By utilizing innovation to computerize processes, smooth out activities and further develop client commitment, organizations can productively get done with jobs, saving time and assets to zero in on center business goals. This can likewise prompt expense investment funds and further developed client commitment through quicker reaction times and improved client encounters. Eventually, organizations can situate themselves for long haul progress in their ventures by embracing advancements that robotize redundant cycles. Quite possibly the best practice I've found for finding what cycles can be computerized is to direct an intensive evaluation of all business cycles to distinguish regions that are monotonous, tedious and inclined to blunders. Archiving each undertaking, delineating the interaction stream, and investigating bottlenecks can give important experiences into where robotization can be executed. Also, investigating programming arrangements that robotize different errands can be useful.

5. Center around consumer loyalty.

Consumer loyalty is critical to scaling a business. Ensure you are conveying a great item or administration that addresses the issues of your clients and surpasses their assumptions. One method for deciding if your item or administration addresses your clients' issues is by gathering input. Studies, online audits and criticism structures are significant apparatuses for social event client data. Dissecting this input routinely is vital for seeing where upgrades can be made.

One more move toward further developing consumer loyalty is by giving fantastic client assistance. Guarantee that your workers are thoroughly prepared and fit for dealing with requests or grievances. I additionally suggest offering motivations like limits or prizes for steadfast clients.

6. Deal with your funds shrewdly.

Scaling a business requires capital, yet dealing with your funds carefully is fundamental. Foster a financial plan, track costs and search for potential chances to lessen expenses and increment income.

7. Remain consistent with your qualities.

At long last, remaining consistent with the guiding principle that drove you to begin your business in any case is fundamental. Pioneers are essential in driving their association toward their main goal and vision. As far as I can tell, the best chiefs comprehend that guaranteeing their business mirrors their qualities is urgent to accomplishing those targets.

All in all, how might you decide whether your organization is remaining on track? One way is by laying out clear objectives and consistently observing the advancement of those objectives to comprehend assuming your group's endeavors line up with the organization's main goal and values. I prescribe doing whatever it may take to lay out a culture of responsibility and straightforwardness, as this assists work with trusting and honesty among colleagues. It's likewise vital to pay attention to input from representatives and clients to check how well the business is meeting those qualities.

As far as I can tell, there is no one size-fits-all way to deal with scaling a venture. Every business is extraordinary and requires a customized approach that thinks about its special objectives, values and culture. Nonetheless, by zeroing in on the key variables illustrated above, you can get yourself in a good position and for accomplishing practical development over the long haul.

Chapter 8: Tax Planning Strategies

Understanding Tax Deductions and Credits

Nobody needs to pay more in government taxes than they need to — and you shouldn't. There are 2 things that assist with figuring out what you truly owe: tax deductions and tax credits.

What is a tax credit?

A tax credit is a sum that can be deducted straightforwardly from your tax bill or, at times, added to your tax discount. For instance, in the event that you have a $1,000 note and guarantee a $250 credit, you owe $750.

What is a tax deduction?

A tax deduction decreases your taxable pay. Also, less pay = less taxes. Assuming you guarantee a $1,000 deduction, it implies you don't pay tax on that $1,000. On the off chance that you're in the 22% government tax section, you just saved $220. Not at all like tax credits, which you can guarantee regardless of how you record your taxes, every year you need to choose whether to organize your tax deductions on the Structure 1040 Timetable A (a significant piece) or take what's known as the standard deduction.

The standard deduction is a dollar sum set every year by the IRS that is deducted from your gross pay. For tax year 2023, the standard deduction is $13,850 for single filers and hitched couples recording independently, $20,800 for heads of family, and $27,700 for wedded couples documenting together and qualifying widow(er)s.1 Thus, in the event that a solitary filer procured $50,000 in 2023, they can take away $13,850 from their pay, and their government personal taxes will be determined in view of $36,150 of taxable pay.

On the off chance that a filer can guarantee deductions — like the ones we'll educate you concerning beneath — that amount to more than their standard deduction, they may rather decide to organize. That is exclusively drilling down their deductions as opposed to taking the standard deduction to decrease their taxable pay by that bigger sum. Assuming your organized deductions would amount to not exactly the standard deduction, organizing probably won't help you.

Contingent upon whether you organize or take the standard deduction, the following are 11 tax breaks that might actually diminish your last tax bill or increment your discount. Simply recollect, numerous deductions and credits have qualification necessities in light of your pay, documenting status, and different variables, so survey IRS rules and talk with a tax counselor on your own circumstance.

Regardless of whether you organize:

1. Children and wards credits

Assuming that you're monetarily liable for a youngster, relative, or other individual, these words could lessen your tax bill or even raise your discount sum.

The Kid Tax Endlessly credit for Different Wards permit you to guarantee tax credits for every one of your passing wards. If your altered gross pay (MAGI) — your gross pay with specific changes — is under $400,000 if recording mutually or $200,000 with some other documenting status for 2023, this could mean $2,000 per kid under 17 (toward the finish of 2023) or $500 per other ward. In any case, on the off chance that your MAGI is over those sums, you could in any case meet all requirements for a halfway credit.

The Kid and Ward Care Credit covers childcare costs, or the consideration of a mate or parent who isn't intellectually or genuinely ready to really focus on themselves, while you work or search for work. It's worth up to $1,050 for one kid or ward, or up to $2,100 for at least 2 youngsters or wards, contingent upon your pay.

Assuming you've taken on a kid and caused reception costs, the Reception Credit can get you up to $15,950 back on your taxes for that tax year assuming you're inside pay limits.

2. Retirement reserve funds deductions and credits

Putting something aside for your future self can take care of sooner than you'd naturally suspect.

To start with, any pre-tax commitments you make to a work environment retirement account, for example, a 401(k) or 403(b), may diminish your taxable pay. On the off chance that you add to a conventional IRA and make not exactly as far as possible, you might have the option to deduct some or those commitments at tax time as well, contingent upon your recording status and, on the off chance that you're documenting mutually, whether your companion is covered by a retirement plan at work.

Remember: There are yearly cutoff points to the amount you can add to a work environment retirement plan and an IRA. However, not at all like work environment retirement plans, you have until the tax recording cutoff time to make last-minute IRA commitments that could decrease your earlier year's taxable pay. Write in your schedules during the current year: April 15, 2024 (April 17 assuming you live in Maine or Massachusetts).

There's likewise the Saver's Credit, a tax credit worth up to half of your commitment to a working environment retirement plan or IRA. Through this credit, you could get up to $2,000 assuming you're hitched recording mutually or $1,000 for all others. A few necessities: being 18 or more established, not being an understudy, and not being guaranteed as another person's reliant.

3. Medical services investment funds deductions

Putting something aside for qualified clinical costs in a wellbeing investment account (HSA) or an adaptable spending account (FSA) could diminish your gross taxable pay as well. Assuming the record is through your boss' advantages, you might make pre-tax commitments straightforwardly from your check. On the off chance that you open the record yourself since you have a HSA-qualified wellbeing plan, your commitments are tax-deductible at the government level regardless of whether you organize. Very much like with an IRA, HSAs have yearly commitment cutoff points and you're permitted to add to them up until Tax Day.

4. Advanced education deductions and credits

Educational cost expenses and understudy loans could cut you down the remainder of the year, however they could surrender you a leg at tax time. Up to $2,500 of interest paid on qualifying understudy loans might be deducted from your gross taxable pay whether you take the standard deduction, for however long you're inside as far as possible, you're not hitched recording independently, and neither you nor your life partner can be guaranteed as wards.

You may likewise fit the bill for 2 instruction related tax credits, however both have pay limits. In the event that you're in your initial 4 years of higher ed, going to in some measure half-time, and chasing after a degree or other qualified qualification, the American Open door Tax Credit could shave up to $2,500 off your tax bill. The Lifetime Learning Credit permits you to guarantee up to $2,000 on qualified educational and training related costs paid toward undergrad, graduate, and expert degree courses during the tax year. However, you can't take both of these credits for similar understudy or similar costs in a similar tax year.

In the event that you're putting something aside for advanced education costs in a 529 school reserve funds plan, those commitments are not governmentally tax-deductible. Be that as it may, you might have the option to deduct them from your state taxes, contingent upon your arrangement and where you live.

5. Energy proficiency credits

More green for being green. You could guarantee 2 different tax credits for energy-productive home redesigns. The Energy Proficient Home Improvement Credit could surrender you back to $1,200 for energy-saving enhancements, like updates to warming, cooling, or added protection, in addition to up to $2,000 for qualified heat siphons, biomass ovens, or biomass boilers. Assuming that you introduced an energy-creating framework, like sun powered chargers, windmills, or geothermal intensity siphons, you could possibly guarantee up to 30% of that venture back through the Private Clean Energy Credit.

Did you take the jump toward another electric vehicle in 2023? Contingent upon your pay and the sort, cost, and maker of the vehicle, you may be qualified for up to $7,500 off your tax bill through a spotless vehicle tax credit. Utilized electric vehicles are presently qualified for a tax credit as well: On the off chance that you bought a pre-owned EV or energy unit vehicle from an authorized vendor for $25,000 or less, you're not guaranteed as a ward on another person's tax return, and you're inside as far as possible, you might be qualified for a credit equivalent to 30% of the deal value up to $4,000.

For 2023, purchasers can guarantee these credits at tax time, yet beginning in January 2024, qualified purchasers can move the credit straightforwardly to showrooms as an initial installment at the hour of procurement. This is permitted no matter what a purchaser's tax obligation is.

6. Pay and work credits

Normally, your profit has a major impact on your tax bill size. Yet, on the off chance that you're under as far as possible, you might have the option to take the Acquired Personal Tax Credit. Planned for low to direct workers, this credit could assist you with guaranteeing anywhere between a couple hundred to two or three thousand bucks, contingent upon whether you have children and in the event that you're recording alone or mutually with a companion. Different kinds of revenue, like speculation pay, may affect your qualification as well.

Except if you own a business, your work costs probably won't be tax-deductible. Yet, there are a few special cases. On the off chance that you're a teacher who burns through cash on study hall supplies and other fundamental costs, you might have the option to deduct up to $300 in 2023. Check assuming you're qualified — and keep those receipts.

7. Property and speculation misfortune deductions

Tax season can assist you with offsetting what you've acquired with what you've lost. If your home, vehicle, or different things were harmed in a governmentally pronounced debacle, for example, a tropical storm or twister, you might have the option to deduct what protection didn't cover. (You could be qualified for other monetary assistance as well.)

Concerning financial planning, you pay taxes on acknowledged venture gains — any protections you've sold for a benefit. Be that as it may, assuming you've likewise gotten rid of ventures during the year at a bad time, you might deduct those misfortunes from your capital increases, diminishing the sum you'll be taxed on. In the event that you lost more than you acquired in a year, you might deduct up to $3,000 ($1,500 assuming you're hitched recording independently) from your common pay as well. Lost more? You could extend the rest to use in ongoing years.

On the off chance that you organize:

8. Altruistic gift deductions

Money related gifts to qualified charitable associations can be tax-deductible, contingent upon your pay. The equivalent goes for non-monetary rewards. So that pack of garments or cleansed toys both count. Different gifts could incorporate home merchandise, books, old vehicles, even stocks and securities, however pay cutoff points could contrast when you give resources rather than cash.

Peruse the IRS rules cautiously or counsel a tax guide prior to deducting given things. The IRS could believe they're worth short of what you do. Deductible garments and home products, for instance, should normally be in great utilized condition or better. In the event that any given thing in this classification isn't to some extent in great utilized condition and you've deducted more than $500 for it — then, at that point, you'd require a certified examination and Structure 8283.2 Track all gave things and their qualities.

9. Personal clinical and dental cost deductions

Revealed or personal clinical costs, particularly shock ones, can be excruciating. (Secret stash, anybody?) Luckily, if these amount to over 7.5% of your changed gross pay, you might have the option to deduct them on your taxes. This is valid for your companion's and wards' medical services benefits as well, including specialist or dental specialist expenses, clinic care, solutions, and even enslavement therapy. Look at this rundown of qualified costs.

In the event that you have a handicap, or your life partner or a ward does, related costs, for example, openness home enhancements or devoted care, could likewise be deductible. For those unemployed because of a long-lasting incapacity, you may likewise be qualified for the Credit for the Older or the Handicapped.

10. Home, city, and state deductions

Assuming you own your home (or a subsequent home, fortunate you) and have a home loan, you might have the option to deduct the interest you paid over time, in addition to different charges, for example, prepayment expenses or even some late installment expenses. Whether your house is a house, townhouse, loft, barndominium, or past, your buy year and home loan sum influence the amount you can deduct.

Contingent upon where you reside, you might be paying nearby or state taxes. In the event that you organize, you're permitted to deduct a blend of your local charges and either your state and nearby personal taxes or your state and neighborhood deals taxes, up to $10,000 (or $5,000 for those wedded and recording independently).

11. Betting misfortune deduction

Roll the dice and hope for the best, you pay some, you deduct some. Indeed, you're on the snare for taxes on betting rewards, yet in the event that the spaces, cards, or lotteries weren't in that frame of mind at different times, you can deduct misfortunes up to the sum that you won from betting. No successes? Sadly, you will not have the option to deduct your misfortunes, however essentially you'll have no extra taxable pay. You'll simply should be that individual in the gambling club requesting receipts

Maximizing Tax-Efficient Investments

Step into a reality where expanding returns is a workmanship, where shrewd investment methodologies crash into cunning tax arranging. This world, old buddy, is that of tax-efficient money management. From the surface, it might seem like some other domain of money, yet look carefully and you'll find it's a unique advantage, an overlooked yet truly great individual that has the influence to shape your monetary predetermination significantly.

Contributing isn't just about the amount you acquire; it's likewise about the amount you get to keep. What's more, that, dear peruser, is where the sorcery of tax-proficiency becomes possibly the most important factor. For the unenlightened, tax-efficient money management is a methodology that expects to limit tax risk and expand after-tax returns. It's really not necessary to focus on sidestepping taxes. Bear in mind, however, about making the most out of the tax rules to allow your investments to fill in the absolute most productive manner.

We'll dig into the stray pieces of what taxes mean for your investments, why tax-proficiency is essential to expanding your profits, and the techniques that can make you a maestro of tax-efficient money management. Whether you're a carefully prepared financial backer or an inquisitive novice, there's an abundance of bits of knowledge looking for you. So fix your safety belt, set out to think critically, and how about we set out on this elating excursion into the universe of tax-efficient financial planning!

Understanding Taxes in Investment

Before we can become amazing at tax-efficient money management, we should initially meet the "mythical serpent" we're attempting to tame - taxes. Dear peruser, taxes and investments resemble two divine bodies in steady gravitational draw. Each move one makes impacts the other, making a complicated dance that can have significant ramifications on your profits. Permit me to direct you through this complex expressive dance.

At its center, the effect of taxes on investment returns is very direct - the more you cover in taxes, the less you keep in your pocket. Basic, isn't that so? In any case, recollect that, we're in a vast dance, and things are not generally as straightforward as they appear.

Presently, envision this - you're a space explorer, and your investments are planets you're investigating. Every planet has its own environment, and that climate is the tax that you should explore. A few planets - we should call them the 'Personal Tax' and 'Capital Increases Tax' planets - have thick environments that can make routes precarious. Annual tax, dear explorer, is demanded on the premium pay from your investments. Capital increases tax, then again, backs its head when you sell an investment for a benefit. Explore shrewdly, for these planets can altogether eat into your profits in the event that they are not taken care of accurately.

Then there are different planets - we should call them 'Stocks', 'Securities', 'Common Assets', and 'Land'. Every one of these investment planets is taxed in an unexpected way. For example, long haul capital additions from stocks and shared reserves have different tax rates, and land investments can offer exceptional tax allowances. Understanding how every one of these investment planets is taxed, assists you with getting ready for the excursion and capitalize on your investigation.

In our enormous dance of taxes and investments, understanding is power. The more we comprehend the taxes that influence our investments, the more we can explore their impact, and the nearer we get to amplifying our profits. Thus, dear peruser, we should proceed with our excursion with this newly discovered information, knowing that we're one bit nearer to becoming amazing at tax-efficient financial planning.

The Significance of Tax-Efficient Financial planning

We should pause for a minute, dear peruser, to consider effective money management a long distance race, a long, twisting street towards monetary success. On this street, taxes carry on like somewhat of a headwind, dialing us back, adding obstruction, and frequently slipping through the cracks until we understand how much harder we need to attempt to keep up with our speed. Similarly as a long distance runner trains to endure and decrease this headwind, we, as financial backers, should gain proficiency with the specialty of tax-efficient financial planning to oversee and relieve this tax opposition.

Presently, you might ask, why is tax-proficiency so significant? Indeed, envision this. Suppose you have two investment portfolios, An and B. Both convey similar gross returns, however An is tax-efficient, while B isn't. Short term, the distinction could appear to be insignificant, scarcely a scratch on a superficial level. Be that as it may, long term, similar to the patient turtle in Aesop's tale, the tax-efficient portfolio A bit by bit pulls ahead, its benefits intensifying over the long haul.

For what reason does this occur? Indeed, recollect that headwind we discussed? In portfolio B, the tax headwind is more grounded. It reliably diminishes the net return, prompting less capital that can be reinvested. After some time, this makes a compounding phenomenon, and the outcome is a huge slack in the development of portfolio B contrasted with its tax-efficient partner.

In any case, don't carelessly believe me. We should take a hypothetical model. Assume we have $10,000 to put resources into two portfolios, An and B. Both procure a gross return of 7% per annum, however portfolio A, being tax-efficient, has an after-tax return of 6.5%, while B has an after-tax return of 5.5%. North of 30 years, with yearly compounding, Portfolio A would develop to around $79,000, while B would just reach about $57,000. That is an incredible $22,000 contrast! A seriously observable total, right?

Understanding and applying tax-efficient money management standards isn't tied in with beating the tax framework or tracking down provisos. It's tied in with knowing the guidelines of the game, and afterward playing the game too as you can inside those standards. It's tied in with being an educated and keen financial backer, utilizing your insight to pursue choices that are beneficial, yet additionally shrewd and economical for a really long time. Since, in the long distance race of effective financial planning, it's not just about running quick, it's additionally about running shrewdly.

Strategies for Tax-Efficient Investing

Welcome to the Fantastic Chessboard of Tax-Efficient Investing, where each move can either present to you a bit nearer to checkmate, or spot your ruler in risk. Yet, fret not! You're in good company in this game. Here, your handy dandy aide, to assist you with grasping the possible moves, strategies, and strategies that could get you in an ordering position. In this way, we should dig into a portion of the strategies in our playbook - resource area, tax-misfortune gathering, hold versus sell strategies, and the utilization of tax-advantaged accounts.

To begin with, we should think about the craft of resource area, a strategy as sensitive as an expressive dance execution, requiring accuracy, equilibrium, and elegance. With resource areas, we apportion various kinds of speculations across various sorts of records in view of their tax productivity. Consider it orchestrating the pieces on your chessboard in a manner that boosts their assets. For example, ventures that create high taxable pay (like securities) can be put in tax-conceived or without tax accounts, while tax-efficient speculations (like record reserves) can be situated in taxable records. The point? To move effortlessly around the tax entanglements!

Then, we have the shrewdness methodology of tax-mis fortune gathering, much the same as the deft moves of a chess grandmaster transforming a likely misfortune into a strategic benefit. With tax-mis fortune gathering, you can offer speculations that have declined in worth to balance capital additions from different ventures. It's tied in with perceiving that occasionally a retreat can set you up for a superior hostile. In any case, it's essential to be aware of the IRS's 'wash deal rule' while utilizing this procedure.

Pushing ahead, we have the hold versus sell strategies, an inquiry as old as the round of chess itself - to move or not to move? This technique includes settling on determined conclusions about when to sell or clutch a venture. For example, holding a venture for north of a year prior to selling might permit you to pay long haul capital increases tax, which is commonly lower than momentary rates.

At last, we have our fortifications on the chessboard, the tax-advantaged accounts. These are exceptional sorts of records like IRAs, 401(k)s, and HSAs, which offer different tax benefits. Utilizing these records successfully can be compared to sustaining your protections and defending your ruler.

However, recall, dear peruser, each methodology accompanies its own arrangement of upsides and downsides, similarly as each continue on a chessboard opens a few entryways and closes others. Resource area requires cautious preparation and customary audit. Tax-misfortune collecting, while worthwhile, needs exact execution and comprehension of rules. Hold versus sell strategies request tolerance and discipline, and tax-advantaged accounts frequently accompany commitment limits and severe withdrawal rules.

By the way, outfitted with these strategies, you are presently more ready to play the excellent round of tax-efficient investing. Comprehend them, use them admirably, and watch as your ability on the chessboard develops. Prepared for your best course of action? We should continue!

Instruments and Assets for Tax-Efficient Investing

Ahoy, individual pioneers! As we proceed with our excursion through the maze of tax-efficient investing, we end up at the foot of the Pinnacle of Apparatuses and Assets. This lofty construction houses the instruments you want to explore your tax process like an expert map maker. From tax arranging programming that demystifies the tax puzzle to monetary counselors who can direct you like prepared wayfarers, these assets can be your compass and sextant in the immense ocean of tax-efficient investing. In this way, we should lift the sails and adventure further into these waters.

To begin with, how about we unwind the sorcery of tax arranging programming. Envision having an indefatigable copyist, industriously working day in and day out, fastidiously sorting out your monetary records, running complex computations, and assisting you with graphing the most tax-efficient course. That is unequivocally the thing tax arranging programming does! Instruments like TurboTax and TaxAct, among others, bridle the force of calculations and computerized reasoning to make tax arranging as easy as cruising on a quiet ocean. They assist you with upgrading derivations, oversee capital additions and misfortunes, and even give bits of knowledge on what different venture choices can mean for your taxes. Like a specialist pilot, these instruments can control you away from potential tax entanglements and towards tax-saving shelters.

In any case, consider the possibility that you wish for a human touch on your journey. Indeed, enter the monetary consultants, the carefully prepared chiefs of the finance oceans. Their insight and experience can give priceless bits of knowledge into the complicated universe of tax-efficient investing. A monetary counsel can make a customized tax system, taking into account what is happening, your gamble resilience, and your speculation objectives. They can direct you on the when, what, and where of your venture process, guaranteeing you stay on the most tax-efficient course. Generally, they can assist you with exploring the difficult situations and blustery climate that the tax world frequently tosses your direction.

In any case, recall, individual pilgrim, each apparatus and asset accompanies its own arrangement of advantages and impediments. Tax programming, while at the same time being efficient, may not completely take care of incredibly complex monetary circumstances. Furthermore, monetary consultants, while giving customized direction, include some significant pitfalls. Thus, the key is to track down the equilibrium - the ideal blend of instruments and assets that fit your necessities, similar to tracking down the ideal breeze to fill your sails.

In this way, equipped with these devices and assets, you're presently more ready to leave on your tax-efficient investing venture. Tackle them shrewdly, and may they generally steer you towards prosperous terrains.

Presently, will we adventure further into our tax-efficient investing journey? Ahead, we sail!

Contextual analyses: Tax-Efficient Investing in real life

All around me, a valiant swashbuckler! As we explore the completely exhilarating oceans of tax-efficient investing, nothing paints a more clear picture than the stories of those who've cruised these waters before us. Genuine contextual investigations act as our directing stars, lighting our direction with experiences gathered from real excursions. They're our tax-efficient Odyssey, loaded up with legends, key fights, and hard-acquired triumphs. Presently, snatch your spyglass as we investigate these interesting accounts and reveal the valuable illustrations they hold.

Our most memorable story spins around a daring pilot, we should call her Helen. Helen, a careful organizer, consistently watched out for her speculation portfolio. Nonetheless, she didn't really think about the 'tax drag' that snuck away at her profits. It was only after she plunked down with a monetary guide, that she understood the genuine effect of taxes on her profits. Executing a tax-efficient technique, including a mix of tax-advantaged retirement accounts and vital resource areas, she had the option to fundamentally upgrade her after-tax returns. Helen's story highlights the significance of mindfulness and the marvels a very much arranged tax technique can do.

Our next narrative carries us eye to eye with a dauntless traveler, we'll name him Odysseus. Odysseus had a different venture portfolio, however it was the blustery oceans of a market slump that tried his fortitude. With smart exhortation from his monetary counselor, he utilized the procedure of tax-misfortune gathering, changing the slump tide in support of himself. He auctioned off his failing to meet expected stocks, counterbalancing his capital additions, and yet again adjusted his portfolio, all while avoiding the wash-deal rule. Odysseus' adventure features the power of tax-misfortune collecting and its capacity to change likely misfortunes into tax-efficient triumphs.

Our last story acquaints us with Athena, a bold financial backer known for her drawn out venture vision. Athena knew the significance of holding her speculations for over a year to profit from the lower long haul capital increases tax rates. This persistence permitted her to appreciate critical tax reserve funds, changing her venture system into a triumphant long distance race as opposed to a furious run. Athena's story is a demonstration of the force of persistence in tax-efficient investing.

These stories from the tax oceans offer us more than exciting stories; they offer pieces of shrewdness, strategies demonstrated in fight, and a compass directing us towards tax-efficient fortunes. As we diagram our own tax process, we should keep these illustrations near our heart and sail towards a consistently efficient skyline. Presently, prepared to proceed with our undertaking? We should investigate further!

Long-Term Tax Planning

Long-term tax planning is a strategic approach to managing your financial affairs in a way that minimizes tax liabilities over an extended period. It involves thoughtful consideration of various financial decisions and the utilization of legal strategies to optimize tax efficiency. Here are key aspects of long-term tax planning:

1. Investment Strategies:

Tax-Advantaged Accounts: Maximize contributions to tax-advantaged accounts such as 401(k)s, IRAs, and other retirement plans. These accounts offer tax benefits, such as tax-deferred growth or tax-free withdrawals in retirement.

Tax-Efficient Investments: Consider investments with a focus on tax efficiency. This includes strategies like tax-loss harvesting and holding investments for the long term to benefit from lower capital gains tax rates.

2. Estate Planning:

Gift and Inheritance Taxes: Develop an estate plan that minimizes gift and inheritance taxes. This may involve gifting assets strategically, establishing trusts, or taking advantage of the annual gift tax exclusion.

Step-Up in Basis: Understand the implications of the step-up in basis for inherited assets. This can impact capital gains taxes for heirs when selling inherited assets.

3. Income Splitting and Family Planning:

Income Splitting: Explore opportunities for income splitting within the family, especially if there are significant income disparities among family members. This can be achieved through income-sharing arrangements or by taking advantage of income-splitting strategies available in certain tax jurisdictions.

Education Savings: Utilize tax-advantaged education savings accounts, such as 529 plans, to save for children's education expenses. Contributions to these accounts may be tax-deductible, and qualified withdrawals are tax-free.

4. Business Tax Planning:

Entity Structure: Choose the right business entity structure to optimize tax efficiency. Factors such as the nature of the business, size, and future growth plans should be considered. Options include sole proprietorships, partnerships, corporations, and limited liability companies (LLCs).

Tax Credits and Deductions: Identify and take advantage of available business tax credits and deductions. This may include research and development credits, energy efficiency incentives, and deductions for business expenses.

5. Charitable Giving:

Donations and Deductions: Strategically plan charitable contributions to maximize deductions. Consider options such as donor-advised funds or contributing appreciated securities to reduce capital gains taxes.

Charitable Trusts: Explore the use of charitable remainder trusts or charitable lead trusts, which can provide both charitable contributions and potential tax benefits.

6. Tax-Efficient Withdrawal Strategies:

Retirement Withdrawals: Plan the timing and structure of withdrawals from retirement accounts during retirement. This may involve a combination of Social Security benefits, pension income, and withdrawals from tax-advantaged accounts to minimize tax liabilities.

Roth Conversions: Evaluate the benefits of converting traditional retirement accounts to Roth IRAs, especially during years with lower income or tax rates.

7. Tax Law Awareness:

Stay Informed: Stay abreast of changes in tax laws and regulations. Tax laws are subject to change, and being aware of updates can help you make informed decisions and adjust your long-term tax planning strategies accordingly.

8. Health Savings Accounts (HSAs):

Contributions and Withdrawals: Maximize contributions to HSAs, which offer triple tax benefits—tax-deductible contributions, tax-free growth, and tax-free withdrawals for qualified medical expenses.

Long-term tax planning requires a comprehensive methodology that thinks about your whole monetary picture. It's prudent to work with tax experts or monetary guides to foster a modified methodology that lines up with your particular objectives, conditions, and the developing tax scene. Standard audits and acclimations to your arrangement are fundamental as your monetary circumstance changes and tax regulations advance.

Working with a Tax Professional

Working with a tax professional is an important stage in dealing with your funds and guaranteeing consistency with tax guidelines. The following are five central issues to consider while drawing in a tax professional:

1. Expertise and Qualifications:**

Credentials: Pick a tax professional with important qualifications, like a Guaranteed Public Bookkeeper (CPA), Selected Specialist (EA), or tax lawyer. These professionals go through thorough preparation and assessments, guaranteeing they have the essential information and skill to deal with complex tax matters.

Specialization: Think about a tax professional with mastery in your particular requirements. A few professionals have some expertise in individual taxation, while others center around business taxation, global tax, or explicit enterprises. Coordinating their specialization with your prerequisites can prompt more compelling direction.

2. Communication and Accessibility:

Availability: Guarantee that the tax professional is open and accessible when required. Ideal correspondence is vital, particularly during tax season or while confronting basic monetary choices. Explain assumptions about reaction times and accessibility consistently.

Correspondence Style: Pick a professional with a correspondence style that lines up with your inclinations. Whether you favor normal updates, top to bottom counsels, or compact outlines, clear correspondence cultivates a superior comprehension of your monetary circumstance and tax methodology.

3. Compliance and Ethics:

Moral Standards: Select a tax professional who sticks to high moral guidelines. Moral way of behaving is fundamental for keeping up with trust and guaranteeing that your monetary undertakings are taken care of with honesty. Confirm their adherence to professional sets of principles and ask about any expected irreconcilable circumstances.

Consistence Knowledge: Tax regulations are intricate and dependent upon future developments. A learned tax professional stays current with tax guidelines and changes methodologies as needs be. Affirm that the professional shows a guarantee to remain informed about updates and changes in tax regulations.

4. Personalized Approach:

Individualized Guidance: Look for a tax professional who gives customized direction in view of your one of a kind monetary circumstance. Tax arranging isn't one-size-fits-all, and a modified methodology guarantees that your particular objectives and conditions are viewed as in the dynamic cycle.

Understanding Your Objectives: A tax professional ought to find an opportunity to grasp your present moment and long haul monetary goals. Whether you're centered around limiting tax liabilities, anticipating retirement, or overseeing speculations, their recommendation ought to line up with your more extensive monetary objectives.

5. Fees and Transparency:

Charge Structure: Comprehend the tax professional's expense structure forthright. A few professionals charge hourly rates, while others might have fixed expenses for explicit administrations. Straightforwardness about charges and potential extra costs dodges astounds and guarantees that the monetary game plan is obvious all along.

An incentive for Services: Consider the worth given comparable to the expenses charged. A gifted tax professional can offer important bits of knowledge that might offset the expense of their administrations. Assess the general offer and evaluate whether the advantages line up with your monetary objectives.

Working with a tax professional can prompt more educated monetary choices, viable tax arranging, and an inward feeling of harmony. By taking into account their skill, correspondence style, moral guidelines, customized approach, and charge structure, you can fabricate a cooperative and valuable relationship that upholds your drawn out monetary achievement.

While could working with a tax professional be particularly gainful?

Complex monetary circumstances:

In the event that you have various pay sources, own investment properties, or have ventures, the complexities of your funds might profit from professional direction.

Independently employed people:

Exploring business derivations and guaranteeing independent work taxes can be interesting, and a professional can guarantee exactness and streamline your tax benefits.

New to tax regulations:

In the event that you're new to recording taxes or uncertain about ongoing changes in the tax code, a professional can give clearness and guarantee consistency.

Confronting a review:

Having professional portrayal during a review can essentially lessen pressure and guarantee your freedoms are safeguarded.

Chapter 9: Mindset and Habits for Financial Success

Presentation: Human instinct has given the capacity to decide. How those choices are made, notwithstanding, really depends on every person. As a matter of fact, a large portion of us realize that going with certain choices isn't so significant as settling on different choices. In any case, making a mindset that utilizes key reasoning is the main way you will really pursue key choices for vital preparation in all parts of your life.

Fostering a mindset that can lead you forward to financial achievement, as well as outcome in all pieces of life, is the main way you will actually want to procure abundance without acquiring it. Also, presumably the main way you will keep up with your abundance effectively, on the off chance that you in all actuality do acquire it. The right mindset comes from self-assessment, going with choices that are about better wellbeing, further developed information and abilities, and difficult work to make your superior way of life ongoing.

Without the right mindset, an individual doesn't have the strength of character to be the individual the person in question needs to be, to ceaselessly improve or to keep up with those enhancements.

Perhaps, the most troublesome aspect of making the mindset of a tycoon is self-assessment. Self-assessment will be tended to. Without a legitimate and troublesome search inside ourselves, we can't roll out skilled improvement. This is the start of the street to change, and on the off chance that you don't attempt to get this mindset that will lay out new propensities and fabricate character, you essentially won't change. The psyche is our aide. We understand our thought process. We act from what we esteem and accept and we track down values and convictions by handling our involvement with our psyches. In the event that we have a shut mindset, we won't change. The mindset should be laid out as the reason for any advancement throughout everyday life. It should be set to be available to novel thoughts, to individuals who are assorted, and to venturing beyond the safe place.

Seeing Ourselves and Perceiving How Others See Us: When you are prepared to begin a course of progress, there is just a single initial step, and that is a self-assessment. To do this in a strong and dynamic manner, you need to get a few days alone. It is an interaction that you should view in a serious way. It requires profound thoughtfulness. On the off chance that you can't focus on this, then, at that point, you're not prepared to focus on the stuff to create financial wellbeing.

A self-investigation will expect you to get things on paper, to consider, and be as legitimate with yourself as you can. First take some enormous paper and a marker and set up a T outline. Put down on one side everything that hinders expanding a mogul mindset, and on the opposite side, those qualities and abilities that will help with your objectives. Take as much time as is needed. Take a gander at your abilities, the manner in which you work, think, and even eat. Try not to give yourself bogus credits. Tell the truth.

This next part is unique. Contemplate remarks others have made to you throughout the long term. Were a portion of their commendations thought up as a matter of common courtesy? Were a portion of their words extremely broad, something you'd share with anybody? The vast majority make statements that won't cause profound torment for other people. We seldom get reality. Do you stick to a good remark and nestle dependent upon it frequently to attempt to rest easier thinking about what you do? Have individuals let you know what you need to hear, or praised you just to help your spirits or your confidence? What weren't you told? This will take more optional reasoning, however it is significant. Getting self-esteem from others can be an issue, as a result of this very thing.

Then again, on the off chance that you sing a performance and individuals say you worked effectively, yet continue on and don't actually look stunned at your singing, you can likely depend on the reality they were simply being great. In the event that you are bad, who is truly going to tell you? An old buddy is somebody who will get a genuine stomach with you, not mollify you. Have you been called to act in different spots? On the off chance that you compose, do you get rehash clients? Do you get advancements or notices or extraordinary approval from the chief? Consider cautiously about these things and record what you think your associates and loved ones truly think about you?

What about your loved ones? Do they boast about you to other people, or appear to appreciate your conversation? Do they request to get things done with you? Now and again the greatest articulation of someone's thought process is finished by quietness. Is it conceivable to see our own inadequacies? In different examinations about self-discretion, they showed that individuals, as a general rule, generally like to assume more profoundly of themselves than others do. They assume they are more intelligent, more entertaining, famous, and educated. The majority of us could concur with that.

Analyze your hard working attitude. Could it be said that you are late to work frequently? Do you slide when you can, or do you attempt to fulfill all necessities expected of you? Do you uphold those in your family, or not mind? Do you attempt to learn and fill in information persistently? And your interactive abilities? Might it be said that they are rough, adequate, or do you get grievances every once in a while? What does your life partner say out of resentment? It is most likely reality. However in some cases we express things out of resentment just to hurt the other individual; while possibly false, those words are without a doubt near reality.

What about cash? Is it true that you are mindful of where yours goes? Might you at any point speak the truth about how much cash you spend inefficiently? Could it be said that you are focused on saving, being economical, and watching the expense of things rise, and the things you assume you want likewise rise? Do you put on a façade to seem more extravagant than you are? Do you talk like you experience no cash difficulties, when you owe such a huge amount on your Visas that your Mastercards can't be taken care of in all out when the bill shows up? Perhaps you move cash around to cover things, since you are so broadened. Do you spend over your means and disregard talking about funds at home?

And your qualities? Do you say a certain something, and act in an unexpected way? Do you say you esteem saving, yet spend unnecessarily? Do you rationalize or imagine all is well, when it's not? Assess what you accept, and afterward record how you act - - the great and the terrible. Try not to give yourself a pass on anything.

This ought to be a period for getting free from the brain - - an all out clear of the pieces of your life that don't interface with effective reasoning.

What You Don't Realize That You Don't Have the foggiest idea: It's an interesting psyche stunt. We think our cerebrum keeps loads of information, yet nearly - - does it truly? Of the multitude of things there are on the planet to be aware of, we really know very little, and we know nothing about things we have no information on. We close ourselves off to progress and learning, since we assume we have enough. It is rarely enough. Life is loaded up with change, new creations, novel thoughts, and new probabilities. Any time an individual thinks they've arrived at their cutoff in learning, they have halted individual advancement. Learning doesn't mean returning to school. It may very well be taking some expert internet improvement, mastering another expertise, another dialect, an instrument, or basically perusing different books or other understanding material. Assuming that you quit acquiring new data, you will be lost in this day and age. Consider how much the more seasoned ages miss on the off chance that they won't become PC proficient? We become out of date, in the event that we don't persistently learn. Assuming that we are putting away cash, you can get exhortation from a monetary counsel, which is perfect, however that doesn't mean you can overlook your reasonable level of effort to be aware however much you can about his recommendation. Open doors, a brief look at the entire world, and investigating science in an exceptionally specialized and genuine way can be generally gotten from the Web. Never before has the regular individual had such a huge amount readily available. Today you can go on the web and quest for anything and anybody. To think you have learned everything is funny. Nobody will at any point learn everything. Kids today discover a great deal more about utilizing innovation than the typical grown-up, in light of the fact that they see it like a game, another revelation simply ready to be opened. Kid mode makes youngsters more responsive to new and various things, in light of the fact that their regular experience is with new and different learning. Consider how much a youngster advances before he will school, just by connecting with others, watching, and tuning in. Simply consider the amount more we could learn assuming we guarantee a portion of that kid mode conduct back.

The outlook of a tycoon is more similar to that of a youngster's mentality. Their brains are forever open to potential open doors, information, individuals, and thoughts. They seldom close their reasoning until rest catches them. Rest is the solution for cerebrum recovery, so it can start again the following day with crisp handling of new and old data. Rest, sound play, active work, learning new things, and building a psychological file organizer of individuals, their activities, the significance of what they see, and deciphering through the faculties as they travel during each time is an astonishing miracle. Part of achieving the mogul outlook is really resetting our reasoning to that tracked down in youth.

Guarantee Against Chance: One more piece of the self-evaluation is to cause notes of how you to protect the dangers you take. Gambles are whatever that you do or say that have some potential for misfortune. Deficiency of cash, the things you own and esteem. So make another rundown of all you own and esteem. Which would cause sadness and trouble on the off chance that you lost them, or lost their utilization. You could list your wellbeing, your vehicles, home, family, work, life, and information and abilities. Then, at that point, confirm them, in the event that you realize they are guaranteed, yet you know for how much. On the off chance that you don't have great protection against these things, what might occur? Try not to rely upon karma. Wellbeing can be lost in a second, as can life. To assemble an outlook for outcome in arriving at your objective objectives, the stress over misfortune should be gone. It can disappear assuming that you have some sort of protection to safeguard you. Perhaps your protection for employment cutback is you acquiring new abilities on the PC, and knowing how to go into business. Protection that your marriage stays sound might be investing energy alone with your life partner and children habitually.

Everything you can't survive without should be protected by some move that you make. Protection for these should be deliberate. That implies you need to understand what worth everything has for you, and expertise to keep up with that value. Turning into a mogul is a deep rooted business.

There will be mishaps, yet don't think of them as disappointments. Consider each mishap as input from life about how you are doing, and what isn't working. Give a great deal of consideration to them and learn, rearrange, and plan how you will gain from the experience. It could mean impacting the manner in which you work, the speed at which you feel it's important to move toward abundance, or the techniques you use to put away and set aside cash. Recollect that it has required a long investment to bring in your cash and it didn't come simple. So contributing that pay, spending that pay, or anything you conclude to do with it ought not be chosen without investing a similar sort of energy and exertion. Your life needs to change to reflect what you have decided on. At times an individual might reach the place where he needs to admit he simply doesn't have the energy, endurance, or determination to take care of business. The contention is: dial back. Speculations will come around, and you might miss a decent one. That is completely fine. It is smarter to miss a wise speculation than to place cash into one hastily, and without study and information.

A significant part of the time, the greatest misstep made in creating vital mind handling, is grinding away excessively quick. Assuming that you lose what you value, since you're not finding an opportunity to get everything done well, it will set you back more over the long haul. This is a lifetime undertaking you are having with riches. Keep the fervor, the positive progression of energy, and the feeling of disclosure.

Having vital reasoning and an unmistakable mentality before you make changes is essential to making your arrangements, completely finishing them, and pushing down the way toward making 1,000,000 bucks. Knowing why this is significant is shown in the choices we make, the moves we initiate, and the existence we lead. Realizing that misfortunes aren't disappointments, yet things to work harder at, and afterward you do, will give you the lightness to move on the up and up.

Understanding that a self-assessment is basic to seeing yourself in splendid lights, not to cause you to have a discouraged outlook on where you are not, yet to cause you to have an empowered outlook on everything you can do right now to make changes and begin the excursion. Assume a sense of ownership with your own life and your own objectives, since, in such a case that you don't you will be quickly passed up the breezes of the world and you will lose where you are and why you are residing.

Concede that you know very little. Track down a spot to start that will begin immediately to influence the manner in which you think, then act, and afterward oversee life. Disregard making an arrangement to procure your million, until you have slashed, separated your reasoning and remolded it into a solid and successful working machine.

At long last, give protection against misfortune. When you open your entire cerebrum, you will actually want to sort it out.

Overcoming Financial Challenges

Understanding financial challenge

Assuming that you're stressed over cash, you're in good company. A considerable lot of us, from everywhere in the world and from varying backgrounds, are managing financial pressure and vulnerability at this troublesome time. Whether your concerns come from a deficiency of work, raising obligation, unforeseen costs, or a mix of variables, financial concern is perhaps of the most well-known stressor in current life. Indeed, even before the worldwide Covid pandemic and coming about monetary aftermath, an American Mental Affiliation (APA) investigation discovered that 72% of Americans have a focus on outlook on cash at any rate a portion of the time. The new monetary troubles imply that considerably a greater number of us are presently confronting financial battles and difficulty.

Like any wellspring of overpowering pressure, financial issues can negatively affect your psychological and actual wellbeing, your connections, and your general personal satisfaction. Feeling pounded by cash stresses can antagonistically influence your rest, confidence, and energy levels. It can leave you feeling irate, embarrassed, or unfortunate, fuel strain and contentions with those nearest to you, compound agony and emotional episodes, and even increase your gamble of sadness and tension. You might depend on undesirable survival strategies, like drinking, manhandling medications, or betting to attempt to get away from your concerns. In the most terrible conditions, financial pressure could actually provoke self-destructive considerations or activities. Be that as it may, regardless of how miserable your circumstance appears, there is help accessible. By handling your cash issues head on, you can find a way through the financial mess, facilitate your feelings of anxiety, and recover control of your funds — and your life.

Regardless of how hopeless your circumstance might appear right now, there is an exit plan. These procedures can assist you with breaking the cycle, facilitate the pressure of cash issues, and find strength once more.

Tip 1: Converse with somebody

While you're confronting cash issues, there's much of the time major areas of strength for a to contain all that and attempt to go solo. Large numbers of us even look at cash as a no subject, one not to be examined with others. You might have an off-kilter outlook on revealing the sum you procure or spend, feel disgrace about any financial errors you've made, or be humiliated about not having the option to accommodate your loved ones. Yet, suppressing things will just exacerbate your financial pressure. In the ongoing economy, where many individuals are battling through no issue of their own, you'll probably find others are undeniably more comprehension of your concerns.

Besides the fact that talking face-to-face with a confided in companion or cherished one, a demonstrated method for stress alleviation, yet talking straightforwardly about your financial issues can likewise assist you with placing things in context. Hushing up about cash stresses just enhances them until they appear to be outlandish. The straightforward demonstration of communicating your concerns to somebody you trust can cause them to appear to be undeniably less scary.

The individual you converse with doesn't need to have the option to fix your concerns or propose financial assistance.

To facilitate your weight, they simply should work things out without judging or censuring.

Speak the truth about the thing you're going through and the feelings you're encountering.

Talking over your concerns can assist you with figuring out the thing you're confronting and your companion or cherished one might try and have the option to think of arrangements that you hadn't considered alone.

- **Getting proficient exhortation**

Contingent upon where you reside, there are various associations that proposition free directing on managing financial issues, whether it's overseeing obligation, making and adhering to a spending plan, tracking down work, speaking with leaders, or guaranteeing benefits or financial help. (See the "Get more assistance" area underneath for joins).

Whether you have a companion or cherished one to converse with for everyday reassurance, getting useful guidance from a specialist is generally really smart. Connecting is definitely not an indication of shortcoming and it doesn't imply that you've in some way or another flopped as a supplier, parent, or life partner. It simply implies that you're sufficiently wise to perceive what is happening is causing you stress and needs tending to.

- **Address an Authorized Specialist**

BetterHelp is a web-based treatment administration that matches you to authorized, licensed advisors who can assist with melancholy, nervousness, connections, from there, the sky's the limit. Take the evaluation and get coordinated with a specialist in just 48 hours.

- **Take Appraisal**

HelpGuide is client upheld. We might procure a commission on the off chance that you pursue BetterHelp's administrations in the wake of navigating from this site. Find out more

Opening up to your loved ones

Financial issues will more often than not influence the entire family and enrolling your friends and family's help can be essential in making something happen. Regardless of whether you invest heavily in being independent, stay up with the latest on your financial circumstance and how they can assist you with setting aside cash.

Allow them to communicate their interests. Your friends and family are most likely stressed — over both you and the financial strength of your nuclear family. Pay attention to their interests and permit them to give ideas on the best way to determine the financial issues you're confronting.

- **Set aside a few minutes for (economical) family fun.**

Put away standard time where you can appreciate each other's conversation, let off pressure, and disregard your financial concerns. Strolling through the park, messing around, or practicing together doesn't need to cost cash, however it can assist with facilitating pressure and keep the entire family positive.

Tip 2: Take stock of your funds

Assuming you're battling to get by, you might figure you can ease your pressure by leaving bills unopened, staying away from calls from leaders, or overlooking bank and financial records. Yet, keeping the truth from getting what is happening will just exacerbate the situation over the long haul. The initial step to conceiving an arrangement to take care of your cash issues is to detail your pay, obligation, and spending throughout the span of no less than one month.

Various sites and cell phone applications can assist you with monitoring your funds pushing ahead or you can work in reverse by social affair receipts and looking at bank and financial records. Clearly, some cash hardships are simpler to tackle than others, yet by taking stock of your funds you'll have a much more clear thought of where you stand. Furthermore, as overwhelming or excruciating as the cycle might appear, following your funds exhaustively can likewise assist you with beginning to recapture a genuinely necessary feeling of command over your circumstance.

- **Incorporate each kind of revenue.**

Notwithstanding any compensation, incorporate rewards, benefits, provision, kid support, or any interest you get.

- **Monitor ALL your spending.**

At the point when you're confronted with a heap of past-due bills and mounting obligation, purchasing an espresso en route to work might appear to be an unessential cost. Be that as it may, apparently little costs can mount up over the long haul, so monitor everything. Seeing precisely the way in which you spend your cash is vital to planning and concocting an arrangement to resolve your financial issues.

- **List your obligations.**

Incorporate past-due bills, late expenses, and rundown least installments due as well as any cash you owe to family or companions.

- **Distinguish spending examples and triggers.**

Does weariness or a distressing day at work make you head to the shopping center or begin internet shopping? When the children are carrying on, do you keep them calm with costly eateries or takeout dinners, as opposed to cooking at home? When you're mindful of your triggers you can track down better approaches to adapting to them than turning to "retail treatment".

Hope to roll out little improvements. Burning through cash on things like a morning paper, noon sandwich, or split time cigarettes can amount to a huge month to month cost. While it could be preposterous to deny yourself each little delight, eliminating superfluous spending and tracking down little ways of diminishing your day to day consumption can truly assist with opening up additional money to take care of bills.

- **Dispense with motivation spending.**

At any point seen something on the web or in a shop window that you just needed to purchase? Imprudent purchasing can wreck your spending plan and maximize your Mastercards. To end the propensity, take a stab at making a standard that you'll stand by seven days prior to making any new buy.

- **Ease off of yourself.**

As you audit your obligation and ways of managing money, recall that anybody can get into financial troubles, particularly on occasions such as this. Try not to blame this so as to recuse yourself for any apparent financial missteps. Offer yourself a reprieve and spotlight on the perspectives you have some control over as you hope to push ahead.

At the point when your financial issues go past cash

At times, the foundations for your financial troubles might lie somewhere else. For instance, cash inconveniences can come from issue betting, extortion misuse, or a psychological wellness issue, for example, overspending during a bipolar hyper episode.

To forestall similar financial issues repeating, it's basic you address both the hidden issue and the cash inconveniences it's made in your life.

Tip 3: Make an arrangement — and stick to it

Similarly as financial pressure can be caused by an extensive variety of various cash issues, so there are a similarly extensive variety of potential arrangements. The plan to resolve your particular issue could be to live inside a more tight budget, bring down the loan cost on your Visa obligation, check your web based spending, look for government benefits, go into chapter 11, or to get another line of work or extra type of revenue.

Assuming you've taken stock of your financial circumstance, disposed of optional and motivation spending, your outgoings actually surpass your pay, there are basically three decisions open to you: increment your pay, bring down your spending, or both. How you approach accomplishing any of those objectives will require making an arrangement and completely finishing it.

- **Recognize your financial issue.**

Having taken stock, you ought to have the option to obviously recognize the financial issue you're confronting. It is possible that you have a lot of Visa obligations, insufficient pay, or you overspend on superfluous buys when you feel worried or restless. Or on the other hand maybe, it's a blend of issues. Make a different arrangement for every one.

Devise an answer. Conceptualize thoughts with your family or a confided in companion, or counsel a free financial directing help. You might conclude that conversing with charge card organizations and mentioning a lower financing cost would assist with tackling your concern. Or on the other hand perhaps you really want to rebuild your obligation, wipe out your vehicle installment, cut back your home, or converse with your supervisor about staying at work past 40 hours.

Set your strategy in motion. Be explicit about how you can completely finish the arrangements you've formulated. Maybe that implies cutting up Mastercards, organizing for a new position, enlisting at a neighborhood food bank, or selling things on eBay to take care of bills, for instance.

- **Screen your advancement.**

As we've all accomplished as of late, occasions that influence your financial wellbeing can happen rapidly, so it's vital to survey your plan routinely. Are a few viewpoints working better compared to other people? Do changes in loan fees, your month to month expenses, or your time-based compensation, for instance, mean you ought to overhaul your plan?

- **Try not to go off track by mishaps.**

All of us are human and regardless of how tight your plan, you might wander from your objective or something startling could end up crashing you. Try not to thrash yourself, yet refocus at the earliest opportunity.

The more point by point you can make your arrangement, the less weak you'll feel over your financial circumstance.

Tip 4: Create a month to month budget

Whatever your plan to ease your financial issues, setting and following a month to month budget can assist with keeping you on target and recapture your feeling of control.

Remember ordinary costs for your budget, like food and the expense of making a trip to work, as well as month to month lease, home loan, and service bills.

For things that you pay yearly, for example, vehicle protection or local charge, partition them by 12 so you can save cash every month.

In the event that is conceivable, attempt to figure surprising costs, like a clinical co-pay or solution charge assuming that you fall wiped out, or the expense of home or vehicle fixes.

Set up programmed installments any place conceivable to assist with guaranteeing bills are paid on time and you keep away from late installments and financing cost climbs.

- **Focus on your spending.**

In the event that you're experiencing difficulty covering your costs every month, it can assist with focusing on where your cash goes first. For instance, taking care of and lodging yourself and your family and keeping the power on are necessities. Paying your Mastercard isn't — regardless of whether you're behind on your installments and have obligation assortment organizations bothering you.

Continue to search for effective cash saving tips. The majority of us can find something in our budget that we can take out to assist with getting by. Consistently survey your budget and search for ways of managing costs.

- **Enroll support from your mate, accomplice, or children.**

Ensure everybody in your family is pulling in a similar bearing and comprehends the financial objectives you're pursuing.

Tip 5: Deal with your general pressure

Settling financial issues will in general include little advances that receive benefits over the long run. In the ongoing monetary environment, it's improbable your financial challenges will vanish for the time being. In any case, that doesn't mean you can't make strides immediately to facilitate your feelings of anxiety and track down the energy and genuine serenity to more readily manage difficulties in the long haul.

- **Get rolling.**

Indeed, even a little customary activity can assist with facilitating pressure, support your temperament and energy, and work on your confidence. Hold back nothing in general, separated into short 10-minute explodes assuming that is simpler.

- **Practice an unwinding strategy.**

Carve out an opportunity to loosen up every day and offer your psyche a reprieve from the consistent stress. Thinking, breathing activities, or other unwinding methods are brilliant ways of easing pressure and reestablishing an equilibrium to your life.

- **Try not to hold back on rest.**

Feeling tired will just expand your pressure and pessimistic idea designs. Tracking down ways of working on your rest during this troublesome time will help both your psyche and body.

- **Help your confidence.**

Properly or wrongly, encountering financial issues can make you feel disappointed and affect your confidence. Be that as it may, there are a lot of other, additional remunerating ways of working on your healthy identity worth. In any event, while you're battling yourself, helping other people by chipping in can build your certainty and simplicity, stress, outrage, and nervousness — also help a worthwhile motivation. Or on the other hand you could invest energy in nature, gain proficiency with another ability, or partake in the organization of individuals who value you for what your identity is, as opposed to for your bank balance.

- **Eat good food**.

A sound eating regimen wealthy in organic product, vegetables, and omega-3s can assist with supporting your temperament and work on your energy and viewpoint. Furthermore, you don't need to spend a fortune; there are ways of eating great on a careful spending plan.

- **Be appreciative of the beneficial things in your day to day existence.**

At the point when you're tormented by cash stresses and financial vulnerability, concentrating on the negatives is simple. While you don't need to disregard reality and imagine all is great, you can pause for a minute to see the value in a cozy relationship, the magnificence of a nightfall, or the adoration for a pet, for instance. It can offer your psyche a reprieve from the steady stressing, assist with supporting your mind-set, and facilitate your pressure.

Developing a Positive Money Mindset

Positive money mindset is a term you have likely heard being thrown around a great deal. Yet, what is it as a matter of fact? Also, how would you get to develop it?

Our relationship with money assumes an enormous part in characterizing our financial prosperity. Developing a positive mindset is something other than collecting riches. Developing a positive relationship with money permits you to develop and encounter financial opportunities.

Luckily, developing a positive money mindset is an excursion that anybody can leave on, no matter what their ongoing financial circumstance. Embracing the right mindset can change our convictions, perspectives, and ways of behaving around money, at last making us ready for a more prosperous and satisfying financial future.

We need to direct you toward that way of overflow, financial opportunity, and prosperity. In this article, we investigate reasonable tips that you can use to assist you with developing a positive money mindset.

1. How about we start by searching internally

Before we get to developing, first we need to figure out what is now there. What I mean is that you really want to do a smidgen of self-reflection and figure out the ongoing convictions, ways of behaving, and mentalities you hold with respect to money.

This step is really significant as it permits you to recognize the restricting convictions you might have learned and gotten all through your life that adversely influence your funds and financial choices.

Perhaps growing up there was very little money to go around and you were dependably in financial endurance mode. You might have grown up feeling that that is the way things are, that you generally must be in endurance mode. However, that may not be reality. Truly, it might make you have a world view limited by fear with regards to money.

Becoming mindful of your convictions about money is a continuous interaction. It requires an eagerness to be straightforward with yourself. Be patient and merciful with yourself as you uncover and inspect these convictions, and be available to testing and supplanting them with additional engaging ones.

2. Challenge Those Restricting Convictions

When you have those restricting convictions written down, time to challenge them and turn them around. This is the way to approach the entire cycle:

Pick one conviction from the ones you recorded.

Ask yourself, is this conviction in view of verifiable proof or past private encounters? Are there any models or cases that conflict with this conviction? What might occur on the off chance that I let go of this conviction? How can this conviction keep me away from arriving at my financial goals?

Search for proof that demonstrates to you that restricting conviction is really a restricting conviction. Pay attention to digital recordings that share examples of overcoming adversity, search out good examples who have accomplished what you need financially, and pay attention to their excursion. Doing this assists you with moving your viewpoint.

Whenever you have done a touch of foundation work, presently it is the right time to rework those convictions. For instance, assuming you believe that money is difficult to acquire, reevaluate that and presently avow that money streams to me effectively and openly.

Make the stride, asserting that money streams to you effectively isn't sufficient, sad to report. You must do whatever it takes to guarantee that money really does truly stream to you without any problem. This might imply that you begin leveling up your abilities, or that you start the discussion of expanding your compensation.

Encircle yourself with people who have a positive money mindset and who support your development either straightforwardly or by implication. Participate in networks, go to occasions, or join bunches that pay attention to individual budget and financial strengthening. Interfacing with similar people can give motivation and support as you challenge and defeat your restricting convictions.

3. Teach Yourself

I don't believe that there is a more grounded point than this one, go out there and attempt to gain some new useful knowledge about various parts of money. To check them out, look into best planning practices to assist you with getting going. Need to assemble your investment funds propensity? Do your own exploration and you may simply learn about Chumz, an application that has planned investment funds to accommodate your way of life (saying).

There are plenty of assets out there that are free and you can take advantage of them. This incorporates Twitter pages, Instagram pages, webcasts, and Youtube channels just to make reference to a couple.

4. Center around the positive

This is the way this all works out;

Rather than harping on what you need or any financial limits that you might have, you direct your consideration toward the assets, open doors, and gifts you as of now have. This overflow mindset frees you up to conceivable outcomes and draws in more financial overflow into your life.

At the point when you value what you have, it creates a feeling of fulfillment and satisfaction. This builds up the conviction that you have enough and more financial overflow is conceivable.

Zeroing in on the positive parts of your financial circumstance, like your financial accomplishments, progress, or shrewd money choices, fabricates certainty and makes a feeling of strengthening. Recognizing your financial successes, regardless of how little builds up the confidence in your capacity to oversee money really and pursue sound financial choices. This certainty enables you to make a positive move towards your financial goals.

At the point when you center around the positive, you foster an open doors and arrangements mindset as opposed to harping on your financial difficulties. You begin seeing possible open doors for development, pay age, or venture. This mindset frees you up to effective fixes and assists you with moving toward financial obstacles with a critical thinking mindset.

5. Clear financial goals

I can't count the times that we have underscored the significance of having clear financial goals. This goes just to show how significant they really are. Having clear goals provides you with a feeling of lucidity, the greater clearness you have the better of an opportunity you will have of swimming in considerations of financial overflow.

Financial goals assist you with feeling in charge of your financial circumstance. Say you want to build your pay. Having an unmistakable objective implies that you will have enunciated moves toward assisting you with arriving. When you play out each step, you're inclined to come by positive outcomes.

Positive outcomes build up and show you that hello, there is sufficient and I'm fit for getting it.

Developing a positive money mindset is a strong undertaking that can change your financial life and in general prosperity. By intentionally moving your considerations, convictions, and ways of behaving around money, you can make a mindset that draws in overflow, development, and financial achievement. All through this article, we have investigated different systems to assist you with doing precisely that.

As you progress forward with your excursion to develop a positive money mindset, recollect that it is a nonstop course of development and self-disclosure. Show restraint toward yourself, practice self-empathy, and commend your advancement en route.

Building Sound Financial Habits

Building sound financial habits is an essential step towards accomplishing financial prosperity and long haul dependability. Developing positive ways of behaving around budgeting, saving, money management, and obligation the executives can prompt a safer financial future. Here are key stages to building sound financial habits:

1. Budgeting and Following Expenses:

Make a Budget: Lay out a reasonable budget that frames your pay, fixed costs (like lease or home loan installments), variable costs (like food and diversion), and investment funds objectives. A budget fills in as a guide for dealing with your cash really.

Routinely Track Expenses: Screen your spending consistently to guarantee you stay reasonably affordable for you. Use applications or budgeting apparatuses that arrange your costs, making it simpler to distinguish regions where changes might be required.

2. Emergency Asset and Savings:

Construct a Crisis Fund: Focus on building a secret stash to cover surprising costs, for example, hospital expenses or vehicle fixes. Expect to save three to a half year of everyday costs to give a financial wellbeing net during unanticipated conditions.

Robotize Savings: Set up programmed moves to an investment account to make saving a steady and easy habit. Robotizing investment funds guarantees that you reliably add to your financial objectives.

3. Debt Management:

Make an Obligation Reimbursement Plan: In the event that you have extraordinary obligations, foster a reimbursement plan. Focus on exorbitant interest obligations and think about combination choices. Laying out an arrangement assists you with gaining ground toward becoming obligation free.

Try not to Gather Pointless Debt: Exercise alert while utilizing charge cards and assume obligation just when fundamental. Try not to gather obligations for unimportant buys to keep up with financial steadiness.

4. Investing for the Future:

Begin Early: Start effective money management for the future as soon as could be expected. Accumulating revenue helps you out when you give your speculations time to develop. Exploit business supported retirement records and individual retirement accounts (IRAs).

Differentiate Investments: Broaden your speculation portfolio to oversee risk. Think about a blend of stocks, bonds, and different resources in view of your gamble resilience and financial objectives.

5. Regular Financial Checkups:

Survey Financial Goals: Lead ordinary financial exams to evaluate your advancement toward financial objectives. Change your budget, reserve funds, and venture methodologies depending on the situation. Customary assessments assist you with remaining focused and adjust to changes in your financial circumstance.

Check Credit Reports: Get and audit your credit reports consistently. Guarantee that the data is precise, and address any disparities quickly. A decent record as a consumer is fundamental for getting great credit terms and loan costs.

6. Continuous Learning and Education:

Remain Informed About Finances: Keep yourself informed about financial issues, remembering changes for charge regulations, speculation systems, and individual budget best practices. Ceaseless learning enables you to settle on informed choices and adjust to advancing financial scenes.

Look for Proficient Advice: Consider talking with financial counselors or duty experts for customized directions. Proficient exhortation can give bits of knowledge into complex financial circumstances and assist you with settling on all around informed decisions.

By integrating these vital features into your financial habits, you can construct a strong starting point for a safe and prosperous financial future. Developing these habits takes time and consistency, so be patient and remain focused on your financial objectives.

Staying Motivated On The Path To Financial Freedom

Staying motivated on the path to financial freedom is pivotal for long haul achievement. Creating financial momentum and accomplishing financial objectives require consistency, discipline, and flexibility. Here are methodologies to assist you with remaining motivated:

Remain Trained and Objective Situated

Remaining motivated and trained while chasing after financial freedom requires responsibility. One way to deal with staying committed is to rehearse objective setting, separating major objectives into more modest objectives that depend on reachable targets. For instance, to save $1,000 in 90 days, break your greater objective of setting aside cash into a progression of month to month stages, setting benchmarks every month as you inch nearer to accomplishing your ultimate objective. This assists with energy and improvement while moving towards your ideal outcome.

Attach Your Objectives to an Unmistakable Thing

One frequently neglected method for achieving this is to attach your objectives to a substantial thing, for example, a reserve funds container or ledger. Imagine yourself with it while arranging out what you want to do today and watch as your little commitments add up.

Having this visual portrayal can be only what you really want on days when you feel unmotivated and searching for a reason not to set aside cash. Taking responsibility for financial objectives is the most vital move towards understanding those fantasies - that remaining trained will assist you with accomplishing!

Remain Taught

Consistently teaching yourself about individual budgets is urgent in remaining motivated and restrained as you seek after financial freedom. Obviously, this begins with knowing how to plan and put down stopping points for yourself.

As you endeavor toward financial autonomy, you really must know where your cash is proceeding to recognize regions where you can scale back spending. There are various ways that you can financially plan your cash, so investigate those choices and track down a way that works for you.

Assuming you are one who likes to contribute, keep awake to date on current market drifts so you face no huge challenges that could set you back a truckload of cash. As you keep on remaining educated and taught about individual budgets, you will pursue informed choices and stay away from exorbitant missteps, which will at last assist you with accomplishing your objectives.

Compare Cash to your Time

Whether you make the lowest pay permitted by law or $100 60 minutes, we as a whole exchange time for cash. Spending less cash is one method for accomplishing more noteworthy financial autonomy. Be that as it may, while you're battling to cut costs, one method for remaining motivated is to comprehend how long your cash sets you back.

For instance, assuming you're playing with the possibility of a $50 buy, consider the amount of your time it would take to make back that $50. How far could that put you behind? Might you want to invest that energy getting that thing?

Contemplating cash concerning minutes/hours of your life can assist you with practicing some limitation without really thinking about purchases or superfluous buys. In the event that you feel like it would be an exercise in futility, it's presumably a misuse of cash, as well.

Observe Little Wins en route

Accomplishing financial freedom can be a long and troublesome excursion, and it's not difficult to become deterred in the event that you just gander at the outcome. You can push your inspiration and force along by celebrating minor triumphs en route.

Put forth feasible momentary objectives, for example, taking care of a Mastercard or expanding your month to month investment funds by a specific sum. At the point when you accomplish these targets, find opportunity to perceive your achievements and

reward yourself .

As a prize for staying with it, give yourself a little treat or enjoy a most loved action. This will help you in keeping up with your inspiration and discipline, as well as making the excursion to financial autonomy more agreeable.

Foster an Activity Plan

Fostering an arrangement with practical goals is significant. Begin by defining momentary goals that are reachable, for example, saving a specific level of every check or taking care of the obligation inside a certain time period.

Then, put forth longer-term goals for retirement investment funds or different goals connected with financial autonomy. Having an arrangement will assist with keeping you propelled and on target to accomplishing your financial goals.

Make a Spending plan

As I would see it, making a spending plan is a fundamental stage toward accomplishing financial freedom. Your spending plan ought to incorporate the entirety of your pay and costs, including things like lease/contract, utilities, food, transportation, diversion, and reserve funds.

By following your spending and recognizing regions where you can scale back, you can let loose more cash to put toward your financial goals.

Put resources into Yourself

Putting resources into yourself is one of the most incredible ways of accomplishing financial autonomy. This could mean returning to school to procure a degree or confirmation that will build your acquiring potential, mastering another ability that could end up being useful to you start a second job, or just finding an opportunity to foster your individual budget information and skill.

Foster Areas of strength

Regardless of how serious you are about your funds with your bookkeeping sheets and number crunchers, you really want motivation to mind. This is where your "why" can assist you with remaining inspired. It tends to be your kryptonite to stalling, your inspiration required for progress.

This "why" of yours can be as senseless or as serious as you maintain that it should be. Any explanation would function as long as it impacts you and keeps you inspired. Maybe you have for a long time needed to open a tabletop game bistro or a solopreneurship. These fantasies require a lot of your cash to get everything rolling. This can be your "why".

Being focused while seeking after financial freedom doesn't mean carrying on with a dull life by the same token. It's tied in with tracking down the right equilibrium. In the event that you are burning through an excess of cash right now and don't have any idea where it's going, halting abruptly won't help. It must be a gradual change. This is the means by which that "why" can assist you with continuing onward.

Play around with it

Becoming involved with the pressure and stress that accompanies taking a stab at financial independence is simple. However, remember to mess around with it. Life is excessively short not to partake in the excursion and arrive at your goals.

Reward yourself for achieving little strides en route, or have some time off from zeroing in on your funds sporadically and accomplish something that gives you pleasure. Celebrate achievement regardless of how little it could be. Partaking in the excursion will make your experience a lot simpler and seriously fulfilling.

Put forth Unambiguous Financial Goals for Progress

While seeking after financial freedom, defining explicit and quantifiable goals can be a vital calculation remaining roused and restrained. As indicated by a concentrate by TD Ameritrade, people who put forth unambiguous financial goals save two times however much the individuals who don't.

Putting forth unambiguous goals can assist you with keeping on track and inspired by giving you an undeniable objective to pursue. Furthermore, keeping tabs on your development toward these goals can assist you with remaining responsible and change your activities if necessary.

For instance, on the off chance that your goal is to put something aside for an initial investment on a house, set a particular sum you need to save every month and keep tabs on your development. Seeing your improvement toward your goal can assist with keeping you roused to save.

Keep in mind, accomplishing financial freedom is an excursion that requires discipline and determination. By putting forth unambiguous goals and keeping tabs on your development, you'll be en route to financial achievement.

Balance Spending Now and Putting something aside for What's to come

My close buddy once told me, "Spend half of your cash like you will pass on tomorrow; spend half of it like you will kick the bucket in 60 years." I've kept these "useful tidbits" in my sub-conscience since I originally heard them since it holds a huge example that I appreciate helping myself to remember.

While it's essential to zero in on the aftereffect of your financial plans, getting deterred or worn out en route is simple. This is particularly evident if the majority of your well deserved cash goes to your reserve funds, business, and venture accounts, leaving none for things that you appreciate. To battle this, you'll have to track down the right harmony between having the option to invest a portion of your pay on things that you appreciate and on things that would assist you with accomplishing financial freedom. By and by, I've followed a 50-30-20 split where I distribute half of my pay for my requirements, 20% for my reserve funds and ventures, and 30% for my needs.

Begin Keeping tabs on your Development

Keeping tabs on your development toward financial freedom is the main move toward remaining inspired and trained while seeking after this goal. Put forth unambiguous goals and track that you are so near accomplishing them.

This will provide you with a reasonable picture of where you stand and give unmistakable proof of your triumphs en route. Following can likewise assist with keeping you propelled on the grounds that it compels you to defy your advancement or scarcity in that department.

Center around the Higher perspective

While chasing after financial autonomy, my best tip is to continuously check the master plan out. I find it accommodating to help myself to remember why I'm doing this: For what reason is financial autonomy critical to me? What is it that I need to accomplish once I arrive at my goal? Pondering potential life altering events and how they can decidedly help my future aides keep me inspired and trained. You can address any gloomy feelings or weakness you might encounter while pursuing financial freedom by placing them into viewpoint: to make a drawn out change, transient penances could need to be made, so it merits watching out for the award.

Taking a gander at the master plan supports the significance of what you're doing and advises you that any momentary endeavors are having a genuine effect toward accomplishing long haul rewards.

Be Available

Each expert excursion encounters dim times, particularly while seeking after financial autonomy. Celebrating minor triumphs and achievements can move you along through troubles and difficulties.

Zeroed in on our essential goal, we frequently disregard our everyday achievements without acknowledging them. Zeroing in on the award shouldn't keep us from commending our everyday expert triumphs.

Construct an Emotionally supportive network

Building an emotionally supportive network is my best way to stay spurred and trained while seeking after financial freedom. Circle yourself with people who have comparable goals and will uphold each other in remaining on track. That could be your family, companions, or even a web-based local area.

Having an accomplice or gathering to consider you responsible is urgent. It will assist you with remaining roused and trained. Furthermore, you can utilize bunch talks and computerized stages to examine venture systems and financial exhortation and support one another.

Online people groups can likewise be a fast asset for data and backing. There are heaps of individual budget and financial freedom bunches where you can bond with individuals who are about growing a strong financial foundation.

With the ideal individuals in your corner and a bunch of sensible targets, you can crush and blossom with the way to financial freedom.

Put forth yourself Miniature Goals en route

Accomplishing financial freedom is a long distance race, not a run. It will require a very long time to finish your essential goal, which makes it hard to remain fixed on the present.

In any case, many key achievements exist along the way, and it very well may be profoundly persuasive to have momentary goals to accomplish. This could incorporate finishing up your backup stash, saving a certain amount of your pay, arriving at a particular reserve funds rate, or even being reliable in your investment funds propensities. In a perfect world, put forth goals you can accomplish in something like a little while, making a need to keep moving.

Whatever your miniature goals, by setting them in any case, you boost the likelihood of progress while at the same time giving yourself something to go for in the quick term, assisting with keeping you on target.

Track down a Financial Responsibility Pal

Having somebody to sympathize with and consider you responsible for keeping up with your forceful reserve funds rate is so significant! My responsibility amigo and I keep each other on target: we give standard updates about our advancement and consider each other answerable for persistently endeavoring toward our financial opportunity goals. This has made me more not set in stone, however it has likewise made a significant connection between us that is a lot further than only the funds.

Chapter 10: Creating a Long-Term Financial Freedom Plan

Setting Long-Term Goals

Whether you're hoping to purchase your own place, resign serenely, or go on an outing that could only be described as epic - laying out long-term financial goals can assist you with succeeding.

Be that as it may, when financial plans are extended and charges need paying, setting cash to the side for what's in store is far from simple or easy - and is much of the time the keep going thing on our psyches.
Our long-term desires are frequently overlooked as we deal with our everyday funds.
Be that as it may, having something to pursue can assist you with keeping on track, become more aware of your spending, and empower you to arrive at your goals.

What are long-term financial goals?

Long-term financial goals are those 'higher perspective' costs that will require at least 5 years to accomplish. For example, eventually, you could have to:

- put down a store on another home
- go on an outing that could only be described as epic
- reserve your kid's schooling

- take a lifelong break
- become obligation free
- resign early
- go into business

These goals regularly include more cash than transient goals (like structure a secret stash or putting something aside for a vacation). Be that as it may, with the right devices and information, they can be accomplished - and be extraordinary for you and others.

The advantages of having long-term financial goals

Laying out a long-term financial objective could:

assist you with turning out to be more careful about how you spend your cash

assist you with keeping on track

give an internal compass and inspiration

Step by step instructions to set and accomplish long-term financial goals

It's never too soon to set up a long-term plan - the prior you set them up throughout everyday life, the more reasonable and feasible they can be.

1. Envision your objective

Anything your financial objective is, ensure you're enthusiastic about it. It should be something that persuades and motivates you.

For instance, in the event that it's putting something aside for a house store, imagine what claiming your own home may be like. Where might you reside? How might you brighten it?

Maybe you're needing to take care of your understudy loan or escape obligation. Envision what it could feel like to drop that load from your shoulders.

In the event that you're expecting to resign early, imagine yourself carrying on with a more adaptable way of life and be doing something you've for a long time needed to do. Our retirement agenda shows you a few little goals you might need to consider, contingent upon your age, to get to where you need to be.

2. Make your objective explicit and quantifiable

What is it that you need to accomplish? What amount do you really want? When do you really want it?

While making an objective, it assists with restricting it down and gives however much detail as could reasonably be expected, so you can keep tabs on your development and commend the little wins.

Our reserve funds objective mini-computer can provide you with a thought of a reasonable time span to pursue.

The greatest long-term financial objective for the vast majority is setting aside sufficient cash to resign. assists you with working out your projected retirement pay and whether you're on track to accomplish the retirement way of life you'd like.

3. Incorporate the sum into your financial plan

A financial plan is an arrangement for what's coming in and what's going out. You let your cash know where to go, rather than pondering where it went - assisting you with focusing on spending. Utilize our spending plan arranging instruments to help.

On the off chance that you have the HSBC UK Portable Banking application, you'll find cash the executives instruments to assist you with planning, develop your cash and accomplish your financial goals. For instance, our Equilibrium After Bills show you the amount you might have left for the month ahead, when booked bills (standing requests and Direct Charges) are considered.

Assuming that you feel you're spending excessively, take a gander at what you can change. These ordinary spending hacks can assist you with setting aside cash - giving additional assets to put towards your future.

There will be days when you go over financial plans - yet that is fine. Having a strategy can assist you with managing mishaps and carry you nearer to your long-term goals.

4. Think about effective money management as long as possible

When you have cash to save, a bank account is by and large seen as a protected method for saving. Notwithstanding, financing costs can go all over. At the point when they're low, the premium you acquire on your investment funds may not be exactly the pace of expansion. This implies the cash you save purchases you less over the long haul.

In the event that you can leave your cash immaculate for somewhere around 5 years, contributing is another choice - particularly for long-term goals.

Ventures - like assets, offers, securities and different resources - could possibly increment in esteem after some time than cash in a bank account. Be that as it may, no speculations are without hazard, and you could get back short of what you put in.

Market vacillations are ordinary - having a secret stash to return to, prior to beginning a longer-term plan, can assist with decreasing the need to plunge into your ventures.

Adjusting Your Plan as Circumstances Change

Adjusting your monetary plan as circumstances change is a pivotal part of dependable and successful monetary administration. Life is dynamic, and unforeseen occasions or changes in needs might require alterations to your monetary technique. Here are key contemplations for adjusting your plan:

1 Survey your spending plan routinely

The initial step to adjusting your financial plan is to routinely survey it. Preferably, you ought to do this something like one time per month, or at whatever point you have a tremendous change in your pay or costs. This will assist you with perceiving how your real spending and saving analyzes your planned financial plan, and distinguish any regions where you want to make changes. You can utilize a bookkeeping sheet, an application, or a paper layout to record and survey your spending plan.

2 Focus on your requirements and needs

The subsequent stage is to focus on your necessities and needs. Needs are the fundamental costs that you should pay to make due and capability, like lease, food, utilities, transportation, and protection. Needs are the optional costs that you can live without, for example, amusement, feasting out, leisure activities, and travel. At the point when your circumstances change, you might have to change your spending on your needs to oblige your necessities. For instance, in the event that you lose your employment, you might have to scale back your needs and spotlight on taking care of your bills and building a rainy day account. On the off chance that you receive a pay increase, you might need to dispense a portion of your additional pay to your reserve funds and speculations, and some to your needs.

3 Change your pay and costs

The third step is to change your pay and costs as per your needs and objectives. Assuming your pay diminishes, you might have to track down ways of lessening your costs or increment your pay. For instance, you can arrange lower rates with your specialist co-ops, drop superfluous memberships, look for more ideal arrangements, or sell undesirable things. You can likewise search for part time jobs, independent work, or different types of revenue. Assuming your pay builds, you might need to expand your reserve funds and speculations, or pay off your obligation quicker. You can likewise indulge yourself with a portion of your needs, however be mindful so as not to overspend and crash your financial plan.

4 Set practical and adaptable objectives

The fourth step is to define reasonable and adaptable objectives for your spending plan. Objectives are the particular results that you need to accomplish with your cash, like putting something aside for a get-away, purchasing a house, or resigning early. They assist you with remaining spurred and zeroed in on your financial plan. Nonetheless, when your circumstances change, your objectives may likewise change. You might have to change your timetable, sum, or need of your objectives, or even make new ones. For instance, on the off chance that you have a child, you might need to put something aside for their schooling, or on the off chance that you face a crisis, you might have to utilize a portion of your investment funds to cover it. The key is to be reasonable about what you can manage and adaptable about how you can accomplish it.

5 Track and assess your advancement

The last step is to follow and assess your advancement on your spending plan. This will assist you with perceiving how well you are adhering to your spending plan, that you are so near your objectives, and what your circumstances are meaning for your funds. You can utilize different devices and strategies to follow and assess your spending plan, like receipts, bank articulations, applications, or online mini-computers. You can likewise utilize markers, like your total assets, your relationship of debt to salary after taxes, or your reserve funds rate, to gauge your monetary wellbeing. You ought to follow and assess your spending plan something like one time per month, or on a more regular basis in the event that your circumstance changes often.

Continuously Educating Yourself

Continuously educating yourself is a strong and fundamental part of individual and expert turn of events. With regards to financial prosperity, continuous learning furnishes you with the information and abilities expected to settle on informed choices, adjust to evolving conditions, and make long haul progress. Here are key justifications for why ceaseless schooling is urgent in the domain of individual accounting:

1. Staying Informed About Financial Trends:

Financial business sectors, guidelines, and monetary circumstances are dynamic. Persistent instruction empowers you to remain informed about the most recent patterns, guaranteeing that your financial choices depend on exceptional data. This information assists you with exploring changing economic situations and pursuing key venture decisions.

2. **Adapting to Advancing Expense Laws:**
   - Charge regulations go through standard changes, influencing how people deal with their funds. Nonstop training on charge guidelines permits you to streamline your duty arranging procedures, recognize expected allowances, and guarantee consistent with the most recent regulations. This information can prompt huge financial reserve funds.

3. Enhancing Speculation Literacy:

Contributing is a complicated field with different instruments and systems. Persistent training in venture literacy enables you to arrive at all around informed conclusions about resource designation, risk the executives, and portfolio enhancement. Understanding venture choices assists you with building a strong and custom fitted speculation portfolio.

4. Optimizing Individual Planning and Cash Management:

Nonstop training in individual accounting assists you with refining your planning abilities and cashing the executives' methods. Finding out about compelling planning devices, methodologies to pay off past commitments, and brilliant ways of managing money permits you to pursue informed decisions that line up with your financial objectives.

5. Building a Solid Starting point for Financial Literacy:

Financial literacy is the foundation of sound financial navigation. Constant training in financial literacy covers points like figuring out credit, overseeing obligation, and going with informed decisions about reserve funds and ventures. A solid financial literacy establishment is essential for accomplishing and keeping up with financial prosperity.

6. Adopting New Advancements and Tools:

The financial scene is affected by innovative progressions. Ceaseless training assists you with keeping up to date with new financial innovations, applications, and instruments that can improve your financial administration capacities. Embracing these developments can prompt more proficient planning, money management, and financial preparation.

7. Navigating Life Transitions:

Life altering situations, like marriage, being a parent, or retirement, bring new financial contemplations. Nonstop schooling sets you up to really explore these advances. Whether it includes refreshing your bequest plan, changing protection inclusion, or anticipating instructive costs, continuous learning guarantees that you are good to go for evolving conditions.

8. Seeking Proficient Development:

Constant instruction incorporates looking for proficient advancement and valuable open doors, like certificates, studios, or courses connected with individual budgets. Improving your abilities and information can open ways to professional success and increment your ability to settle on vital financial choices.

9. Cultivating a Development Mindset:

Persistent schooling cultivates a development outlook, empowering a readiness to learn, adjust, and embrace difficulties. This mentality is instrumental in defeating financial snags, investigating new open doors, and keeping a proactive way to deal with individual and financial turn of events.

10. Empowering Choice Making:

Information is an amazing asset for strengthening. Consistent instruction enables you to settle on choices with certainty, diminishing the effect of financial pressure and vulnerability. Informed independent direction adds to a feeling of command over your financial future.

Recall that constant training is a long lasting excursion. Whether through understanding books, going to studios, taking web-based courses, or looking for guidance from financial experts, the obligation to continuous learning is an interest in your financial prosperity. It positions you to adjust to changes, profit by amazing open doors, and make supported progress on your financial excursion.

Leaving a Financial Legacy

While moving toward retirement, it's normal for individuals to begin pondering legacy arranging: how they'll be recalled and what they'll abandon. By and large, leaving a legacy for kids, grandkids, or a good cause - and different causes individuals are enthusiastic about - takes cautious preparation and the counsel of a financial organizer.

1. Summer homes Make an Extraordinary Legacy

One major region where individuals can leave a legacy is land, like a subsequent home or a get-away property.

"Some of the time families have a getaway home that makes a big difference to the family," says ensured financial organizer Constance Stone, prime supporter and expert to Ohio-based Venturing Stone Financial, Inc. Be that as it may, people keen on doing so ought to investigate setting up a family restricted organization or a trust for a simpler cycle to move revenue in the property.

As indicated by Stone, abandoning a summer home "can be something magnificent — and furthermore a wellspring of conflict and issues. You need to consider ahead how to set it up so the substance continues onward."

There are likewise some tax cuts for family restricted organizations notwithstanding the capacity to move proprietorship between various kin, Stone adds.

2. Be Clear About Your Family Home and Individual Effects

While excursion land can be a sure thing for a legacy, a similar isn't generally valid for the family home.

""According to Stone, "The family home can be intense, because it's laden with such a lot of feeling." I've seen more family battles over the family home and its things than whatever else."

People thinking about leaving collectibles or anything monetary or nostalgic worth should recall headings for home organizing reports with clear headings for how those things are to be isolated.

"Leave an outline: to give unequivocal things to express relatives, that quick overview will for the most part be regarded, for any period of time it's suggested in the will," Stone says.

3. Make a Recipient IRA

One more method for leaving an enduring legacy is naming youngsters or grandkids as the recipients of conventional Individual Retirement Records (IRAs) or Roth IRAs.

"The best thing you can pass onto kids are Roth IRAs," says Stone, taking note of the assessment cost of conventional IRAs.

Dispersions from Roth IRAs are tax-exempt if the length of the individual who set it up met the five-year holding period for commitments and transformations, she notes. Recipients have five years to take out cash from the record, except if they move the retirement plan record to an Acquired IRA, which permits them to extend appropriations all through their future.

"On the off chance that you don't change it over completely to an Acquired IRA [after the giver dies], then, at that point, you need to take [all the cash in the account] in five years," says confirmed financial organizer Karen DeRose, pioneer behind Illinois-based DeRose Financial Arranging Gathering, of both conventional and Roth accounts.

Individuals deciding to set up recipient IRAs can name different recipients, Stone says. When the giver bites the dust, the IRA is partitioned into discrete records for every recipient and they can get to their assets freely of different recipients. While there is no legitimate breaking point to the quantity of recipients that can be named on an IRA, a few establishments limit that number.

To ensure IRAs are set up accurately to stay away from dissemination punishments or expenses, it's ideal to converse with a proficient duty counsel, DeRose and Stone suggest.

4. Name a Youngster as Recipient for an Annuity

Like recipient IRAs, buying an annuity and naming a youngster as the beneficiary is additionally conceivable. Upon the contributor's passing, the kid then has a revenue stream from annuity installments over their lifetime.

"Since the youngster is more youthful, there will be a greater stream of pay all through their lifetime," says DeRose. "It's one more extraordinary method for ensuring a kid's pay."

5. Utilize Overabundance Conveyances briefly to-Death Life coverage Strategy

Before 2019, when people arrived at age 70 ½, they were expected to begin taking required least dispersions (RMDs) from qualified retirement plans, for example, Individual Retirement Records (IRAs) and 401(k)s (barring a current 401(k) on the off chance that the individual is as yet working). Notwithstanding, the Protected Demonstration, passed in 2019, rolled out a major improvement to RMD necessities by stretching out the age from 70 ½ to 72.

Conveyances start at a specific level of the complete equilibrium between all IRAs and increment as the individual progresses in years.

"Many individuals needn't bother with the cash [from the required distributions] and pivot and reinvest it," DeRose says of her clients. "On the off chance that you don't require it, I tell them, 'How about you remove a portion of it and purchase one moment to-kick the bucket life coverage strategy?'"

These strategies pay out solely after the second companion two or three passes away, making it one of the less expensive disaster protection arrangements, as per DeRose.

For instance, assume there is a hitched couple with two youngsters that buys a $1 million second-to-pass on strategy that expenses somewhere in the range of $20,000 and 25,000 every year and they pay for it with their overabundance disseminations. When the two life partners die, their two kids each get $500,000 from the arrangement.

"Putting the protection payout into an unavoidable trust makes it pay and home tax-exempt, and they're utilizing their giving," DeRose adds. "It's something delightful to do. It's an extraordinary methodology."

6. Gift Deteriorating Stock to Good cause

For those craving to abandon a legacy helping a foundation they're energetic about, a Roth IRA may not be really smart on the grounds that non-benefit, 501(c)3 associations don't profit from tax reductions like people do, says Stone. Nonetheless, bequesting deteriorated stock to a foundation can bring down home charges.

"In the event that you had a ton of stock that deteriorated in esteem that you need to dump, those are frequently taken a gander at for noble cause," she prompts. "It gets the devalued stock out of your bequest, and you don't need to pay charges on that — and the foundation isn't affected by charges, all things considered."

Leaving a legacy isn't about the cash, either, adds Stone, who advocates for a more comprehensive view. For instance, many individuals don't ponder wiping out their homes while they're still around to make it happen.

"Discard the stuff you don't require deserted, so someone else doesn't have to seek after those hard choices," she says. " Kids feel like they're disposing of their people's lives. Accepting for a moment that they're currently going through a significant time, it makes it a lot harder. There's a sensation of culpability."

Another persevering through heritage is lifestyle. " Presumably the best things that my people left me were an appreciation for what I had, and not expecting — or requiring — a lot of material things," Stone says. " Family was very important. Religion and church were huge. Troublesome work was ordinary, and it helped me with developing incredible essential capacities."

Conclusion

Recap of Key Principles

Here is a recap of key Principles examined across different subjects connected with financial freedom and management

1. Financial Goals and Planning:

- Set clear, explicit, and attainable financial goals.

- Foster a thorough financial arrangement that incorporates budgeting, saving, and investing.

2. Budgeting and Cost Management:

- Make a sensible financial plan to follow pay and costs.

- Focus on needs over needs and pursue informed spending choices.

3. Emergency Fund and Savings:

- Construct and keep an emergency fund for startling costs.

- Mechanize investment funds to guarantee predictable commitments.

4. Debt Management:

- Foster an obligation reimbursement plan and focus on exorbitant interest obligations.

- Try not to aggregate pointless obligations and pursue informed choices.

5. Investing Strategies:

- Begin investing ahead of schedule to use the force of accruing funds.

- Differentiate your speculation portfolio to oversee risk.

- Routinely audit and change speculation strategies in light of goals and economic situations.

6. Income and Cost Assessment:

- Survey pay sources and investigate open doors for extra pay.

- Consistently survey and investigate costs to distinguish regions for development.

7. Budgeting for Variable and Fixed Expenses:

- Separate among variable and fixed costs.

- Oversee variable and optional costs dependably.

8. Savings and Cost-Cutting Strategies:

- Carry out cost-slicing strategies to increment investment funds.

- Foster an outlook of purposeful spending and focus on long haul financial goals.

9. Emergency Fund:

- Decide the proper size for your emergency fund in view of everyday costs.

- Keep the emergency fund in a fluid and effectively open record.

10. Handling Surprising Expenses:

   - Be ready for surprising costs by keeping an emergency fund.

   - Consider protection inclusion to alleviate the financial effect of unexpected occasions.

11. Debt The executives Strategies:

   - Concentrate on reimbursement for exorbitant interest obligations. combination choices for working on reimbursement.

12. Risk Resistance and Venture Strategy:**

   - Comprehend individual gamble resistance while fostering a venture methodology.
   - Enhance ventures across various resource classes for the executives.

13. Building a Differentiated Speculation Portfolio:

   - Select a blend of resources to make a differentiated portfolio.

   - Consistently rebalance the portfolio to keep up with the ideal resource distribution.

14. Retirement Planning:

   - Expand commitments to retirement accounts, for example, 401(k)s and IRAs.

   - Consider various sorts of retirement accounts in light of individual conditions.

15. Maximizing Manager Benefits:

- Exploit manager supported benefits, including retirement plans and wellbeing investment accounts.

- Comprehend and enhance manager matched commitments.

16. Creating Extra Revenue Streams:

- Investigate open doors for extra pay through side gigs or recurring, automated revenue sources.

- Put resources into abilities and adventures that can create valuable pay.

17. Strategies for Getting up to speed with Retirement Savings:

- Evaluate and increment retirement commitments if behind on reserve funds.

- Consider deferring retirement or investigating seasonal work to support reserve funds.

18. Continuous Education:

- Remain informed about financial patterns, charge regulations, and speculation strategies.

- Embrace a development outlook and look for open doors for continuous learning.

19. Leaving a Financial Legacy:

- Explain values and goals to direct choices about abundance move.

- Lay out a thorough home arrangement and encourage financial education inside the family.

20. Staying Motivated:

- Put forth clear and reachable financial goals.

- Separate enormous goals into more modest achievements for progressing inspiration.

- Make a dream board to envision financial achievement.

21. Adjusting Your Plan:

- Routinely audit and adjust your financial arrangement in view of changes in conditions.

- Alter budgeting, obligation reimbursement, and speculation strategies depending on the situation.

These standards by and large add to an all encompassing way to deal with financial prosperity and the quest for financial opportunity. Incorporating them into your financial administration practices can assist you with exploring difficulties, gain by open doors, and fabricate a protected and prosperous financial future.

Encouragement for the Financial Journey Ahead

Leaving on the financial journey toward more prominent solidness, security, and at last, financial opportunity is an honorable undertaking. While the way might have its difficulties, vulnerabilities, and snapshots of intricacy, perceiving the meaning of your responsibility and the potential for extraordinary change is fundamental. The following are four vital supportive gestures to inspire and direct you on your financial journey:

1. Embrace the Cycle: The Journey Is just about as Significant as the Destination

As you set out on your financial journey, it's pivotal to embrace the cycle and perceive that the actual journey is an important piece of the experience. The way to financial opportunity is definitely not a straight one; it includes constant learning, variation, and development. Each step you take, whether large or little, adds to your financial prosperity.

Think about this journey as a chance for self-awareness and strengthening. The financial difficulties you experience are not deterrents but instead venturing stones that give important examples. Embracing the interaction permits you to construct strength, upgrade your financial proficiency, and foster an outlook that can explore the intricacies of overseeing cash.

Find an opportunity to praise your accomplishments, regardless of how humble they might appear. Whether it's effectively adhering to a spending plan, laying out a secret stash, or settling on informed speculation choices, every achievement draws you nearer to your financial objectives. Perceive that misfortunes are a characteristic piece of any journey and view them as any open doors to learn and course-right.

Recollect that the most common way of accomplishing financial opportunity isn't exclusively about arriving at an objective however about the development, discipline, and shrewdness acquired en route. Embrace the journey, enjoy the advancement, and stay focused on ceaseless improvement.

2. Cultivate Persistence: Financial Freedom Is a Long distance race, Not a Sprint

Accomplishing financial opportunity is a long distance race, not a run. It calls for investment, steady exertion, and a patient mentality. In a world that frequently esteems moment satisfaction, it's vital to perceive that building a strong financial establishment and arriving at your drawn out objectives take time.

Tolerance is an ideal that serves you well on this journey. It empowers you to remain focused on your financial arrangement, in any event, when confronted with difficulties or slow advancement. Financial achievement isn't about handy solutions yet about making maintainable, thoroughly examined choices that line up with your objectives.

Comprehend that the journey might include forfeits and deferred satisfaction. Whether it's renouncing sure buys, adhering to a spending plan, or persistently trusting that speculations will develop, these activities add to the general objective of financial opportunity. Persistence permits you to climate the inescapable tempests, gain from encounters, and use wise judgment that endure for an extremely long period.

Think about financial persistence as an interest in your future self. The discipline to finish what has been started, in any event, when results are not quick, is an integral asset for long haul achievement. Trust the cycle, remain patient, and spotlight on the gradual advancement that, after some time, prompts critical financial accomplishments.

3. Empower Yourself Through Schooling: Information Is Your Most noteworthy Asset

Information is an impressive device on your financial journey. Enable yourself by effectively looking for schooling and remaining informed about individual accounting, venture techniques, and financial patterns. The more you know, the better prepared you are to pursue informed choices that line up with your financial objectives.

Exploit the abundance of assets accessible, from books and online courses to financial websites and digital recordings. Comprehend the fundamentals of planning, money management, and obligation to the executives. Look into charge regulations and financial arranging standards. Ceaseless schooling upgrades your financial education as well as lifts your trust in exploring the complexities of individual accounting.

Information is a dynamic and developing resource. Remain inquisitive, seek clarification on pressing issues, and be available to groundbreaking thoughts and viewpoints. Organizing with people who share comparative financial objectives can give significant experiences and down to earth guidance. Look for direction from financial experts when required, as their mastery can offer customized answers for complex financial difficulties.

Recall that schooling is a continuous interaction. As financial scenes advance, remaining informed positions you to adjust and settle on all around informed choices. By putting resources into your financial information, you engage yourself to assume command over your financial predetermination and pursue decisions that line up with your qualities and desires.

4. Celebrate Financial Achievements: Recognize and Ponder Progress

Along the financial journey, it's vital to stop and praise the achievements you accomplish. These achievements are not only markers of financial advancement; they address your commitment, discipline, and flexibility.

Recognize the work you put into pursuing positive financial choices and the effect those choices have on your life.

Whether it's taking care of a huge piece of obligation, arriving at a reserve fund's objective, or accomplishing a positive profit from speculations, find an opportunity to consider your achievements. Commend these achievements as unmistakable proof of your obligation to financial prosperity.

Festivity fills in as a strong inspiration. It builds up certain ways of behaving and urges you to keep fixed on your financial objectives. Consider making an achievement agenda or vision board to address your accomplishments and goals outwardly. This substantial wake up call can move you during testing times and act as a demonstration of your financial journey.

Commending achievements isn't just about the objective; it's tied in with valuing the headway made en route. Each financial achievement is a demonstration of your capacity to defeat difficulties, adjust to change, and drive forward chasing a superior financial future. By recognizing and praising these minutes, you develop a positive mentality that fills proceeds with progress.

All in all, the financial journey ahead is a way of development, learning, and strengthening. Embrace the cycle, develop tolerance, enable yourself through training, and praise the achievements en route. Recall that your journey is novel, and each step you take carries you nearer to the financial opportunity and satisfaction you look for. Remain committed, remain tough, and confident in the extraordinary force of your financial journey.